Grammar and Punctuation

by Jay Stevenson, Ph.D.

ALPHA

A member of Penguin Group (USA) Inc.

ALPHA BOOKS

Published by the Penguin Group

Penguin Group (USA) Inc., 375 Hudson Street, New York, New York 10014, USA • Penguin Group (Canada), 90 Eglinton Avenue East, Suite 700, Toronto, Ontario M4P 2Y3, Canada (a division of Pearson Penguin Canada Inc.) • Penguin Books Ltd., 80 Strand, London WC2R 0RL, England • Penguin Ireland, 25 St. Stephen's Green, Dublin 2, Ireland (a division of Penguin Books Ltd.) • Penguin Group (Australia), 250 Camberwell Road, Camberwell, Victoria 3124, Australia (a division of Pearson Australia Group Pty. Ltd.) • Penguin Books India Pvt. Ltd., 11 Community Centre, Panchsheel Park, New Delhi—110 017, India • Penguin Group (NZ), 67 Apollo Drive, Rosedale, North Shore, Auckland 1311, New Zealand (a division of Pearson New Zealand Ltd.) • Penguin Books (South Africa) (Pty.) Ltd., 24 Sturdee Avenue, Rosebank, Johannesburg 2196, South Africa

Penguin Books Ltd., Registered Offices: 80 Strand, London WC2R 0RL, England

International Standard Book Number: 978-1-59257-393-6
Library of Congress Catalog Card Number: 2005923954

14 13 12   10 9 8

Interpretation of the printing code: The rightmost number of the first series of numbers is the year of the book's printing; the rightmost number of the second series of numbers is the number of the book's printing. For example, a printing code of 05-1 shows that the first printing occurred in 2005.

Printed in the United States of America

Note: This publication contains the opinions and ideas of its author. It is intended to provide helpful and informative material on the subject matter covered. It is sold with the understanding that the author and publisher are not engaged in rendering professional services in the book. If the reader requires personal assistance or advice, a competent professional should be consulted.

The author and publisher specifically disclaim any responsibility for any liability, loss, or risk, personal or otherwise, which is incurred as a consequence, directly or indirectly, of the use and application of any of the contents of this book.

Most Alpha books are available at special quantity discounts for bulk purchases for sales promotions, premiums, fund-raising, or educational use. Special books, or book excerpts, can also be created to fit specific needs.

For details, write: Special Markets, Alpha Books, 375 Hudson Street, New York, NY 10014.

Contents

Introduction

English grammar and punctuation can seem pretty complicated, especially if you're not used to thinking in grammatical terms. Grammar and punctuation have to be complicated because we use them in so many complicated ways—to represent and explain concepts, ideas, and plans; communicate; ask for things; persuade; even lie. If you think about it, it's kind of amazing just how much our language does.

As any good worker will tell you, it's important to use the right tools for a job. Grammar is, in essence, a set of rules and conventions that show just what all the different tools in the linguistic toolkit do and how they should be combined into accurate, meaningful phrases, clauses, sentences, and paragraphs.

The basics, fortunately, are fairly simple and may be at least somewhat familiar from English class and from your own experience with language. And after you have the basics down, the rest should come together fairly easily.

For this reason, few people read books on grammar and punctuation from cover to cover. Most have specific problems they want help with. Nevertheless, one of the really nifty things about grammar is the way it all fits together. To really understand any of it well, it helps to have a sense of what it all is. This book is organized both to help people get the big picture of grammar and punctuation to see how their various features work together, and also to be used as a quick reference for questions and problems as they crop up.

The book is divided into two main parts:

Part 1, "Words at Work," covers the rules and conventions of grammar, including all the parts of speech and how they're inflected and combined with one another into phrases, clauses, and sentences. I also identify and sort out common problems and mistakes along the way.

Part 2, "Marks of Distinction," sets forth the rules of punctuation as laid down by the venerable folks at the Modern Language Association. (For more information on the Modern Language Association and the style used in this book, see the following "A Note on Style and the Modern Language Association [MLA]" section.)

Two appendixes follow the chapters. The first is a glossary of grammatical terms; the second is a compendium of common grammatical problems. Lastly, there's an index for quickly locating pretty much everything covered in this book.

In addition, this book is filled with sidebars offering helpful and interesting orts of information on issues related to the topic at hand in the text. These sidebars come in four varieties:

> ### Grammar Jammer
>
> Not all grammar is cut and dried. Here's where you can learn about some of its more interesting and unexpected features.

Parse Words _____

    Read this sidebar for handy definitions of terms employed by grammarians for specialized concepts.

Grammar Rules, OK! _____

    Here's a correct precept in a box. If life were only this simple, we'd always be right!

Margin of Error _____

    These sidebars hold advice on what not to do. If you've ever found yourself straying from the correct path, you may well find the error of your ways in one of these sidebars.

A Note on Style and the Modern Language Association (MLA)

If you're writing for publication, including self-publication and publication for business purposes, you'll want to be consistent in formatting your work and in citing and documenting your sources. For these and other editorial concerns, consult a style guide. "Style" here refers not to writing style, but to editorial style. There are many style guides out there and virtually all professional editors work closely with one of them in editing a manuscript for publication.

The most influential, commonly used styles are those developed by the Modern Language Association (MLA), by the American Psychological Association (APA), and by the University of Chicago Press (UCP). There are many others as well, but the MLA, APA, and Chicago styles are the most widely followed and recognized.

MLA style is intended for scholarly publications as well as for papers submitted in course work. Where appropriate, I have followed it here, because I am most familiar with it as a student and teacher of English. APA style is used for publications in the social and behavioral sciences. Chicago style is commonly used by publishing professionals in various fields.

Acknowledgments

I'd like to thank all my English teachers, from nursery school to post-doc study, for never ceasing to help me use language better. I humbly hope most of them could approve of my efforts in writing this and audaciously dream that this might help others as they have helped me.

Special Thanks to the Technical Reviewer

The Pocket Idiot's Guide to Grammar and Punctuation was reviewed by an expert who double-checked the accuracy of what you'll learn here, to help us ensure that this book gives you everything you need to know about mastering grammar and punctuation in a hurry. Special thanks are extended to Sharon Sorenson.

Trademarks

All terms mentioned in this book that are known to be or are suspected of being trademarks or service marks have been appropriately capitalized. Alpha Books and Penguin Group (USA) Inc. cannot attest to the accuracy of this information. Use of a term in this book should not be regarded as affecting the validity of any trademark or service mark.

Words at Work

Part 1 deals with all the parts of speech and how to make 'em fit together into proper and useful English. For each part of speech, you learn how it can be inflected (change form), how it combines with other parts of speech, and what common problems arise in its use.

Grammar's Working Parts

In This Chapter

- ◆ Why so many people hate grammar
- ◆ Good grammar and good writing
- ◆ The eight parts of speech

Language is the subtlest, most useful tool ever used. Grammar is a set of specifications that show how the tool works and should be used. This tool (language) has different working parts, known as the parts of speech. This chapter introduces each of them.

But first, let's exorcise some grammar demons. We can best deal with these demons by dragging them out into the open and talking about them.

Getting Started with Grammar

Grammar is a set of conventions that structure language. All languages have grammar, so everyone who learns to speak a language learns to use that language's grammar more or less well, whether or not they ever study grammar formally. This means that if you're a human being, you have an innate capacity to make and use language according to grammatical principles, even if you're not consciously aware of them. Practice and study can help make you overtly conscious of the grammar you already use. That consciousness enables you to fix or avoid grammatical mistakes more easily and speak and write with greater clarity. Yeah, grammar!

Yet many people would rather go to the dentist than study the parts of speech. If you have a deep-seated aversion to grammar, think about why. People who aren't crazy about grammar cite many reasons for disliking it, including these:

- Schools sometimes overemphasize grammar.
- Grammar norms can exacerbate cultural and political divisions in society.
- Snobs sometimes harp on grammatical correctness to make ordinary people feel stupid.

Let's think about each of these problems.

Back to School

Sometimes, schools seem to overemphasize grammar. To many students, the rules of grammar loom as arbitrary obstacles that stand in the way of doing the real work of thinking, writing, and learning. After all, writing is a tremendously complicated skill that takes years of practice to develop. Thus, writing, rather than grammar per se, merits more hours of work.

> **Grammar Jammer**
>
> For centuries, Latin grammar was a mainstay of the curriculum for English school boys (enrolled in grammar school), while the teaching of English grammar was modeled after Latin.

In fact, a piece of writing can show weakness for any number of reasons apart from grammatical issues. Poor writing may be banal and simplistic, it may lack coherence, and it may be filled with mis-statements and confusion—all problems difficult for students to overcome without years of reading and study. Some teachers, however (and school curricula), turn to grammar as a quick fix for all kinds of writing problems.

Sometimes this "quick fix" can actually get in the way of learning to write better. In fact, when people try to write about things they don't understand very well, their grammar tends to break down. They often lose track of the rules of grammar when groping for a way to express unfamiliar ideas. In other words, grammar problems are frequently symptoms, rather than causes, of confusion or uncertainty on the part of a speaker or writer.

If you have to write a paper on a really hard, somewhat unfamiliar topic, any difficulty you have in explaining things can lead you to make grammatical mistakes you may not ordinarily make. In cases like this, fixing your grammar may not solve the bigger problem of analyzing and explaining complicated issues. If you have to spend valuable time fixing grammar mistakes in a paper that had more serious problems, you'll probably feel frustrated and dissatisfied.

> ### ❗ Grammar Jammer
>
> Students who have a difficult time reading and writing often find themselves relegated to remedial grammar classes. These classes, sometimes boring and unproductive, may cause students to feel they're being punished for their supposed stupidity, rather than instructed in useful skills.

"Standard" English: Depends on Where You Learned It

Regional and cultural variations affect all languages. Speakers of English speak differently in various parts of the world. American English differs somewhat from British English and from Australian English. Linguistic differences stem from different regions within America as well. In addition, people who come from different ethnic and cultural backgrounds tend to speak English in different ways.

To a degree, variation lends richness to the language, but it can also cause confusion and misunderstanding. In the interest of clarity and consistency, language professionals, including teachers and those in publishing, rely on the idea of Standard English, a universally accepted norm that provides guidance on the proper way to say things.

Language, however, reflects political and cultural values. Different segments of society endorse different ways of speaking and writing as more or less polite, proper, and correct. As a result, certain nonstandard usages garner more criticism as "errors" than do others for reasons that have little to do with consistency and clarity. Consciously or unconsciously, some folks use the "rules" of grammar as excuses for snobbery and prejudice.

Margin of Error

Many native speakers of English have a tougher time learning to correct their grammatical errors than those learning English as a second language because the "mistakes" native speakers make sound correct to them because of the way they learned to speak growing up.

Because their own speech patterns sound right to them, people who grow up speaking nonstandard English often have trouble learning the rules of Standard English. As a result, students who grew up speaking nonstandard English sometimes have more difficulty in English class than many non-native speakers (English-as-a-second-language [ESL] students).

The point is that cultural issues can help explain why good, Standard English grammar is a cakewalk for some students; a difficult but surmountable challenge for others; and a perplexing, impenetrable mystery for still others. If you've been struggling with cultural issues, keep in mind that you may need to come to terms with two different sets of grammar rules: the standard set most people use, and the set you grew up using.

Variations on a Theme

Linguists and English teachers have only recently come to realize that nonstandard regional and cultural variants of the English language have their own particular grammatical structure. In fact, some variants can do things grammatically that Standard English can't do. How about a plural form of the second-person pronoun, *you?* In Standard English, it's simply *you.* There's no distinction between the singular and the plural form.

Some nonstandard English variants, however, inflect the plural form. In the South and in many African American communities, folks say "y'all," as in, "Y'all have a different way of talking." In certain neighborhoods in the Northeast, people say "youse," as in "Youse guys have a different way of talking." Clearly, nonstandard English obeys nonstandard rules of grammar.

The most widely recognized variant of English is "Black English," or Ebonics, as it has come to be called. Ebonics grammar books exist, so take a look at them if you're interested.

Grammar Jammer

A thorny controversy mushroomed in 1996, when the Oakland [California] Public School Board voted to recognize Ebonics both as a legitimate language and as the primary language of most of its African American students. The move, intended to acknowledge and respect the special cultural heritage of African Americans, instead generated fear that focusing on Ebonics would draw energy and attention away from the study and teaching of Standard English.

Upgrade Your Grammar

If your grammar isn't perfect (and whose is?), you can improve it without going back to school. One way is to learn to identify the kinds of mistakes you tend to make. Chances are, you don't do everything wrong, so you needn't re-learn everything. Most people keep making the same specific grammatical mistakes until they learn to fix them. The trick is to find out which sort of mistakes you make.

To determine your common grammar mistakes, do some writing and have someone who really knows how to identify and correct grammatical errors look over your work. If you're already enrolled in a school where English is taught, you should be able to find a qualified teacher easily. You could also test yourself, using a workbook or web page that has exercises on common problems.

In addition, or instead, you could read through the information provided in this book by yours truly. It should give you a good, broad sense of what grammar is all about, as well as offer an intimate look at a whole slew of specifics.

If you've already identified the particular kinds of mistakes you tend to make, you can look 'em up in the index at the back or in Appendix B on common grammar mistakes and read on from there.

Good Wording: The Parts of Speech

In general, words have three characteristics that enable them to function in language:

- ♦ Words have meaning.
- ♦ Words can be joined together into structures such as phrases, clauses, and sentences.
- ♦ Words take different forms that determine their meaning and dictate how they fit together.

These three essential characteristics of words are known as *semantics*, *syntax*, and *inflection*, respectively.

Parse Words _____

Semantics is the realm of language concerned with the meaning of words. **Syntax** refers to the way words fit together into larger structures. **Inflection** is the changing of words into various forms.

Semantics, syntax, and inflection are closely inter-related. To really understand any of them, it helps to have a good grasp of the other two. Fortunately, if you can speak English, you already have a good sense of English semantics and should be ready to wrap your brain around syntax and inflection—the structure of language and the forms of words. These things are pretty much what the rules of grammar are all about.

Grammar Jammer _____

The eight parts of speech apply not only to English grammar, but to most Indo-European languages. The grammarian Dionysis Thrax first identified the eight parts of speech in the first century B.C. when he used them to describe ancient Greek.

All words belong to different parts of speech. These parts of speech—eight of them—make up the different categories that words belong to. The categories depend on the functions the words serve in the language. You can read about each of the eight parts of speech in detail in the subsequent chapters of this book, but for now, here's a list of them, each with an explanation:

- **Nouns.** Nouns name things. It's hard to talk without talking about things. That's why nouns are so useful.

- **Pronouns.** Thanks to pronouns, nouns don't have to be repeated when everyone already knows what they are. *Her* and *she*, for example, are pronouns that come in handy so we don't have to say annoying things such as, "Betty wears a watch on Betty's ankle so Betty can keep track of time when Betty meditates in the lotus position." We *know* we're talking about Betty. "*She* wears a watch on *her* ankle when *she* meditates."

- **Verbs.** Verbs indicate action. Something is always going on, so we need verbs to … to … you name it!

- **Adjectives.** Adjectives describe nouns so we know what things are like. Words such as *green, lumpy, pungent, elastic,* and *hopeful* are adjectives.

- **Adverbs.** Adverbs modify verbs and adjectives. They're the words that typically end in *ly*. In fact, only a few *ly* ending words aren't adverbs: *contumely* is a noun; *surly* and *jolly* are adjectives. One important adverb doesn't end in *ly*, though. It's *well*, which is the adverb form of the adjective *good*.

- ◆ **Conjunctions.** Conjunctions join words and phrases. They include coordinating conjunctions such as *and, but, or, nor,* and *yet* and subordinating conjunctions such as *if, because, although,* and *until.*

- ◆ **Prepositions.** Prepositions such as *at, for, to,* and *with* come before nouns or pronouns to link them to another word in the sentence. In the sentence, "I'll be *at* Ivan's place," *at* is a preposition linking the noun, *Ivan's place* to the verb, *be.*

- ◆ **Interjections.** Grammar has a whole separate category for the kinds of words people shout when they stub their toe or win the lottery. Interjections are words and phrases used as exclamations such as *ouch! Jiminy Cricket, son of a gun,* and *yippie!* Interjections also include many more colorful expressions that I won't repeat here!

Grammar Jammer

To help remember the names of the eight parts of speech, use the acronym "IVAN CAPP" (interjections, verbs, adjectives, nouns; conjunctions, adverbs, prepositions, pronouns).

In addition to these eight parts of speech, some sources recognize one additional part of speech:

◆ **Articles.** Articles come before a noun to show whether it's definite (*the* pistachio, *the* ton of bricks) or indefinite (*a* bookshelf, *an* opportunity).

Words that belong to these eight categories make up all English sentences. Groups of words called phrases can also be categorized as different parts of speech—noun phrases, verb phrases, etc. If you understand what each of these categories represents, you're well on your way to mastering English grammar. Next, you'll need to learn how the parts of speech should and should not be put together to form sentences.

The Least You Need to Know

◆ Many people have unpleasant experiences studying grammar in school.

◆ Some people learn the rules of Standard English more easily than others as a result of regional and cultural variations in speech.

◆ We can categorize words and phrases according to the eight parts of speech: interjections, verbs, adjectives, nouns; conjunctions, adverbs, prepositions, and pronouns.

Chapter 2

Persons, Places, Things, and Stuff: Nouns

In This Chapter

◆ All kinds of nouns: proper, common, collective, noncount, and singular and plural

◆ Direct objects and object complements

◆ Subject, object, and possessive case

You gotta love nouns. These words used for things and stuff are probably the first new words spoken in any language. Nouns are among the first words babies learn when beginning to speak. Our lives are filled with things and concepts that can only be identified by using nouns.

Grammatically speaking, nouns are about as basic and straightforward as words get. Even so, nouns have a few tricky characteristics that give people trouble. And apart from any confusion stemming from nouns themselves, it's good to have a clear understanding of the nominal (nounlike) elements of speech because so many other parts of speech relate to them. So if you're just getting acquainted or reacquainted with grammar, nouns are a good place to start.

This chapter talks about the various ways thing-words and stuff-words can fit into a sentence and how they can change form according to their place and function.

The Renown of Nouns

You've probably heard the maxim that says a *noun* is a word that represents a person, place, or thing. What's more, the things nouns represent include not only ordinary, real, material things such as refrigerators, parking lots, and tree frogs, but also imaginary things, abstract things, and things that are actually stuff. Any word that makes sense with an article (*a, an,* or *the*) in front of it is a noun.

! Grammar Jammer _____

Some nouns derive from other parts of speech. For example, the nouns *transcendence, longing, corruption,* and *five-mile hike* come from the verbs "to transcend," "to long for," "to corrupt," and "to hike." The nouns *falsehood, sanity, roundness,* and *pragmatism* come from the adjectives "false," "sane," "round," and "pragmatic." Conversely, words that start off as nouns can change into other parts of speech. *Doglike, flaky,* and *erroneous* are adjectives made from the nouns "dog," "flake," and "error."

A few aspects of nouns can give some people trouble. Here's a list of the troublemakers in the order in which they're dealt with in this chapter:

- ◆ **Capitalization.** Some nouns, namely proper nouns, get capitalized even when they don't appear at the beginning of a sentence.

- ◆ **Plural forms.** That simple and tidy rule of adding an *s* at the end of a noun when you're talking about more than one thing doesn't always work. Deal with it! Then, once you've got the right form of the noun, how do you know the right verb form that goes with it? Noncount nouns and collective nouns come into play here.

- ◆ **Case.** All nouns take one of three different case forms, *subject*, *object*, or *possessive*. Case forms are crucial for understanding pronouns (discussed in the next chapter).

Parse Words

Subject case is the form of nouns and pronouns that indicates that the noun or pronoun carries out the action described by the verb. **Object case** is the form that indicates that the noun or pronoun receives the action described by the verb. **Possessive case** is the form that indicates that the noun or pronoun possesses a thing or quality.

Common Versus One-of-a-Kind (Proper) Nouns

Nouns can be proper or common. A *proper noun* names a one-of-a-kind thing. For example, your name is a proper noun because you are a one-of-a-kind thing. OK, yes, there is more than just one Pablo or Marcella in the world, but these are names for one-of-a-kind people. No matter how many John Johnsons there are, each John Johnson is a one-of-a-kind thing.

Grammar Jammer

Ever wish we could get by just using nouns alone and chucking all those other annoying parts of speech? In Jonathan Swift's famous satirical fable, *Gulliver's Travels* (1735), the wandering Gulliver visits the land of Balnibarbi, where professors of language are at work expunging everything but nouns from their native tongue. Another group of Balnibarbi professors go even further and propose using actual things instead of words. People would simply carry around with them everything they might want to talk about. Swift is making fun of eighteenth-century academics who wanted to make language more scientific.

Other proper nouns are *Mount Kilimanjaro, Statue of Liberty, Elm Street, Saturn, Japan,* and *Complete*

Idiot's Guide. Notice how they're all capitalized? Capitalize proper nouns whether or not they appear at the beginning of a sentence.

Most nouns, however, are *common nouns*. (No, common nouns are not *im*proper; they're just common.) *Hair, emeralds, keys, time,* whatever—things and stuff that have words for what they are but don't have their own specific names are common nouns.

Things Alone, Things Together— and Stuff

Nouns can be singular, plural, or collective, depending on whether they refer to one thing, many things, or a group of things acting as a unit. A singular noun names a single thing, such as *crayon, elevator,* or *hemorrhoid*. Single nouns, unlike plural nouns, can take the articles *a* or *an*, as in *a kaleidoscope* or *an octopus*. A plural noun refers to more than one thing, such as several *hippopotami* or some *rectangles*.

Rules (Plural) for Making Nouns Plural

Notice the unusual form of the plural noun *hippopotami* in the last sentence of the preceding paragraph? Typically, we make a singular noun into a plural noun just by adding an *s* onto the end of it; thus *crayon* is singular, and *crayons* is plural. Many nouns, however, change to the plural form in other ways. It's possible to have one *child* or many *children*, work in one *medium* or several *media*, get attacked by one ferocious *mouse* or by a whole thundering stampede of *mice*, and hop away on one *foot* or two *feet*.

Kind of complicated, isn't it? What's more, some nouns can become plural without changing at all. In poker, two *pair* beats one *pair*. You might think a flock of *sheep* all descended from a single *shoop*, but that's not how it is. It's a single *sheep*.

Ready for a simple, logical, reliable rule that will tell you which nouns become plural by adding *s* and which nouns become plural some other way? Well, I have bad news: there is no single easy rule.

In fact, the English language has borrowed words from many different languages in the course of its development, and each of those languages has a different way to form plural nouns. Singular/plural forms such as *datum/data* and *antenna/antennae* come from Latin; *ox/oxen* and *man/men* are Germanic.

Regardless of where they come from, these words are part of the English language now.

Many of these plural forms of nouns have to be learned on a case-by-case basis. That's why there's spell check, dictionaries, and English teachers!

Getting Stuff-y

Many nouns refer to groups of things regardless of whether the noun is singular or plural. These are called *collective nouns*. They include words like *conglomeration, committee, party, group,* and *flock*.

Finally, there's one more category for nouns that are neither singular, plural, nor collective. These are *noncount nouns*. Noncount nouns are words for things that can't be counted because they are stuff. *Ooze, richness, chalk, ambition,* and *phlegm* are all noncount nouns. Many nouns, such as *hair, cheese,* and *error,* can be used either as noncount nouns or singular nouns. For example, the word *hair* occurs as a plural noun and also as a noncount noun in the following two sentences:

> The mole on my chin has three hairs growing out of it.

> My hair is brown.

Both collective nouns and noncount nouns generally function as singular nouns as far as the structure of a sentence goes. They take the singular form of the verb when they appear as the subject of a sentence. (You can read about verb forms in Chapter 4. You can read about subjects of sentences in the next section of this chapter.)

OK! **Grammar Rules, OK!** _____

We use two more conceptually useful categories for nouns: abstract and concrete. Concrete nouns refer to tangible things that can be sensed or measured, such as *elephants* and *electrons*. Abstract nouns refer to intangible things such as *beauty, clarity,* and *torpor*.

Subject to Your Consideration

The *subject* is the part of the sentence that performs the action indicated by the verb. In the sentence "Pickles explode." the noun *pickles* is the subject. The subject of any sentence functions as a noun; the simple subject is a noun. The complete subject, as opposed to the simple subject, is a noun together with its modifiers.

In the sentence "Pickles attached to detonators explode." the complete subject includes the noun, *pickles,* and the participle phrase, *attached to detonators,* which modifies the noun. (You can read about participles and participle phrases in Chapter 4.) Note that the word *detonators* is also a noun, but it would be incorrect to say that *detonators* is the subject of the sentence. *Detonators* is part of the complete subject; *pickles* is the simple subject.

Then there are *compound subjects,* which include two or more nouns that function equally as parts of the complete subject. In the sentence "Pickles and potatoes explode." *pickles* and *potatoes* function equally as the simple subject. They are each part of the compound subject, *pickles and potatoes.*

To sum up the way nouns can occur in the subject of the sentence ...

- ◈ A single noun can form the simple subject of a sentence.
- ◈ Two or more nouns can form the compound subject of a sentence.

◆ A noun can be part of a phrase that modifies the simple subject. Such a noun is part of the complete subject but is not *the* (simple) subject.

> ! **Grammar Jammer**
>
> All sentences have subjects, of course, but not all sentences state their subjects. Sentences that are commands often have implied subjects, but not stated subjects. For example, the sentence "Wipe your feet!" has the implied subject *you.*

Object Lesson

Not all nouns appear as the subject or as part of the complete subject of a sentence. Just as a noun can be part of a phrase that modifies the subject, a noun can also be part of a phrase that modifies the verb. But modifiers come later. (You can read all about them in Chapter 5.) For now, the most important kind of noun that doesn't serve as the subject of the sentence is the object. See how symmetrical grammar can be? Nouns can be subjects; nouns can be objects.

On the Receiving End

While the subject of a sentence performs the action indicated by the verb, the *object* of a sentence receives the action or is acted upon. In the sentence "I have the measles." *I* is the subject, and *measles* is the object. In the sentence "Did you make chicken soup?" *you* is the subject, and *chicken soup* is the object.

All sentences have subjects, but not all sentences have objects. Whether or not a sentence has an object depends on if the verb calls for one. As you can read in Chapter 4, some verbs, called *transitive verbs*, raise burning questions of "Who?" or "What?" The object of the sentence provides the answer.

The verb may ask other questions instead, such as "How?" "When?" and "Why?" but the answer to these questions is not provided by the object. "How?" "When?" and "Why?" get answered by adverbs. In contrast, "Who?" and "What?" get answered by nouns. Objects are always nouns.

See if you can pick out which of the following sentences have objects:

> We all lost weight.
>
> Time stood still.
>
> Children usually imitate their peers.
>
> Problems demand attention.
>
> Doris slept soundly.

How'd you do? *Weight, peers,* and *attention* answer the questions "What?" or "Who?" and thus are all objects that receive the action performed by the subjects. *Still* and *soundly* answer "When?" or "How?" and thus are adverbs that modify the verbs *stood* and *slept,* respectively. They're not objects.

❗ **Grammar Jammer**

As a speaker of English, consider your-self lucky that you don't have to worry about whether a book, a board, or a spoon is masculine or feminine. In Romance languages such as French, Italian, and Spanish, nouns are generally categorized by gender—masculine and feminine—to correspond with pronouns and articles that are also either masculine or feminine. Zee Romance grammar, she is a cruel mistress, no?

Do It to It

Ready to get fancy? Let's look at *indirect objects*. When something does something to something else, that "something else" is the indirect object. The indirect object comes after a transitive verb and before the direct object. Remember, the transitive verb raises the question "Who?" or "What?" and the direct object answers the question. The indirect object answers the questions, "To whom?" "For whom?" and "To what?"

In the sentence, "Wendell gave me the rotten potato." *rotten potato* answers the question "What did Wendell give?" and so it is the object. *Me* answers the question "to whom?" and so it is the indirect object.

Notice the subtle difference between the questions "What?" and "To what?" But don't get fooled by the preposition *to* when it appears before a verb instead of before an indirect object. The following sentence has a *to* before a verb:

Wendell gave me something to think about.

Can you identify the object and the indirect object? *Something* is the direct object (answers "What?" after the verb). *Me* is the indirect object (answers "To whom?" after the verb).

Case Studies

Subject and object are known as *case forms* of nouns. The English language has three different case forms: subject, object, and possessive. The possessive case is used for nouns that own or exhibit a thing or quality. It's usually formed by adding 's (apostrophe s) onto the end of the noun. Plural nouns ending in *s* become possessive simply by adding an apostrophe after the *s*.

The use of the possessive case for nouns is redundant (repetitious and wrong) after the words *those of, these of,* and *that of,* so don't do it! It's incorrect to say, "Of all the big noses I've run into, that of Chetley's is the biggest." The correct phrase is "that of Chetley." Makes sense, doesn't it? *That of* indicates possession, so there's no need to indicate possession a second time with a superfluous 's (apostrophe s) after the noun.

Here's something that makes less sense: the use of the possessive case for pronouns (as opposed to nouns) in similar situations is correct. Hence we would say "that of mine," not "that of me."

Getting Possessive

Notice the subtle, but semantically significant, grammatical difference between the following two sentences (both are grammatically correct, but they mean different things):

> We counted all the salamander's toes.

> We counted all the salamanders' toes.

In the first sentence, the singular noun, *salamander's*, takes the possessive case. It means we counted all the toes of a single salamander. In the second sentence, the plural noun, *salamanders'*, takes the possessive case. It means we counted the toes of more than one salamander.

OK! **Grammar Rules, OK!** _____

Here's a cool way to use the possessive case that separates the grammatical elite from everyone else—before participles that pertain to the noun:

No one minded Bridget's going crazy at the game.

What's the Point?

Nouns get inflected (change form) when they take the possessive case. Notice that nouns aren't inflected for the subject or object case. In other words, a noun takes the same form regardless of whether it's used as a subject or an object. Nevertheless, it's good to be able to recognize the difference between subjects and objects. Why? Pronouns!

Pronouns take different subject and object case forms. You can find out all about this and other tantalizing features of pronouns simply by turning the page and letting your intellect run rampant over the next chapter!

The Least You Need to Know

- ◆ Nouns represent people, places, and things— stuff, too.

- ◆ Proper nouns represent proper, one-of-a-kind things and should be capitalized. Common nouns aren't capitalized unless they start the sentence.

- ◆ Not all nouns form their plurals the same way, and no single rule can tell you how to form them.

- ◆ Subjects perform the action indicated by the verb. Objects receive the action.

- ◆ Nouns do not change form for subject or object case, but do change for possessive case, by adding 's (apostrophe s).

Chapter 3

Wildcard Words: Pronouns

In This Chapter

- ♦ Pronouns and pronoun reference
- ♦ Indefinite pronouns
- ♦ Case agreement
- ♦ Reflexive pronouns

Nouns are a good thing, but as with anything else, too much of a good thing is not a good thing. That's why we have pronouns. Pronouns provide a subtle, tactful way to refer to things we've already named with nouns. Say something once, why say it again? You can avoid repeating nouns by using pronouns.

Pronouns are almost like wildcards. You can use them to stand in for any noun you want. Take, for example, the pronoun *it*. *It* can refer to just about anything. Or how about the pronoun *anything?* *Anything* can also refer to just about … well …

The point is, pronouns are pretty darn useful. But they can be tricky, too. Sure, they look like insignificant little words that don't really mean a whole lot on their own, but they carry a lot of grammatical weight, and that's just where the challenge lies. It's important to inflect them properly so they fit in with what's going on in the rest of the sentence.

Pronouns come in several varieties depending on the sorts of nouns they stand for. In addition, many pronouns follow special rules for taking the plural form. Some are reflexive, as we'll see later in this chapter. More importantly, many of them are inflected according to case.

We deal with all these issues in this chapter. But for starters, let's concentrate on the primary, basic role pronouns fill: namely, to stand in for, and refer to, nouns.

Follow the Leader

Wherever there's a pronoun, there should be a noun nearby for the pronoun to refer to. A noun that a pronoun refers to is called the *antecedent*. If there's no antecedent, or if it's not clear which of two or more nouns the pronoun refers to, you'll confuse your reader. In fact, vague pronoun reference is a common problem, as in the following example:

> In the fall, the maple trees turn brilliant red and yellow. That is my favorite color.

Here, it's unclear which noun, *red* or *yellow*, is the antecedent of the pronoun *that*.

> **Margin of Error**
>
> Unclear pronoun reference can be a symptom of unclear speech, writing, or thought. When a pronoun doesn't have a clear antecedent, it's often because a logical step is missing from a description or explanation.

Other common problems of pronoun misuse are faulty case (for example, confusing *who* and *whom*), and number disagreement (for example, confusing *each are* and *each is*). Before looking at each of these—and other—problems with pronouns, it may help to take a sweeping overview of pronoun-kind.

Pronouns on Parade

Brace yourself! Here comes a dazzling array of pronouns, taken out of their natural habitat and divided up into their grammatically significant categories—personal, demonstrative, relative, interrogative, and indefinite.

Personal Pronouns

These pronouns stand in for people and things.

Subject Case	Object Case	Possessive Case	
I	me	my	mine
you	you	your	yours
he	him	his	his
she	her	her	hers
it	it	its	its
we	us	our	ours
they	them	their	theirs

Notice that personal pronouns change form to show possession. For example, the possessive case of *they* is *their* and *theirs*. Because the possessive case indicates possession, there's no need to add *'s* (apostrophe s). In fact, it's incorrect to say *their's* or *theirs's*.

Margin of Error

Here's a classic boo-boo: At some time or another, almost everyone confuses *it's*, which is the contraction of "it is," and *its*, which is a possessive pronoun. The following sentence uses both *it's* and *its* correctly:

It's plain to see, just by looking at the cabinet, that its handle is loose.

Demonstrative Pronouns

These pronouns refer to things.

	Singular	Plural
Things close by	this	these
Things far away	that	those

Relative Pronouns

These pronouns form the links between dependent and independent clauses:

   that, which, who, whom (object case), whose

Interrogative Pronouns

These pronouns ask questions. Note they are the same as relative pronouns, except that they get used in different ways:

   that, which, who, whom (object case), whose

Indefinite Pronouns

These pronouns refer to nonspecific things:

   all, any, each, anyone, anybody, someone, somebody, everyone; everybody, everything, nothing, one, either

Dealing With Indefinites

Indefinite pronouns are a common source of confusion. They often refer to hypothetical situations, so it can be hard to see whether they stand for one thing or many things and whether the thing or things they refer to are masculine or feminine.

We Got Your Number

Nothing and *one* are always singular, as in the sentence "Nothing is bad." *Both*, *few*, and *many* are always plural, as in the adage "Many are called, but few are chosen." But many indefinite pronouns, including *all, any, more, most, none,* and *some,* can be either plural or singular, depending on their antecedents. Compare the following two sentences:

> Some of the chips are broken.

> Some of the dip has broken chips in it.

In the first sentence, *some* is plural; in the second, *some* is singular.

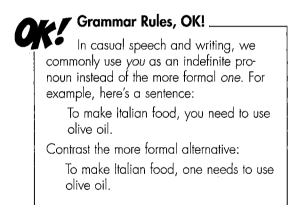

Grammar Rules, OK!

In casual speech and writing, we commonly use *you* as an indefinite pronoun instead of the more formal *one.* For example, here's a sentence:

> To make Italian food, you need to use olive oil.

Contrast the more formal alternative:

> To make Italian food, one needs to use olive oil.

However, *each* and *any* are singular when they are used to specify individuals belonging to a group, as in the sentence "Each of the puppies wagged its tail." Even though *puppies* is plural, *each* is singular and agrees with the singular verb form *is.*

Gender Bender

Here's an odd state of affairs: traditionally, the masculine pronouns *he* and *his* have been used to refer to indefinite pronouns such as *somebody*, *someone*, *everybody*, and *everyone*, regardless of whether or not females are involved. For example, according to this traditional view, the sentence "Everyone got mud on his face." is grammatically correct even if *everyone* refers to a mixed group.

OK! **Grammar Rules, OK!** _____

Generic use of the pronoun *he* to refer to people who may be women is widely considered sexist. So are words such as *mankind* and gender-specific words for occupations such as *stewardess* and *salesman*. Good alternatives are *humankind*, *flight attendant*, and *salesperson*.

Well, things change, even for grammarians. The use of *he* and *his* to refer to individuals, some of whom may be women, is no longer widely accepted. Instead, you can choose from various alternatives:

Everyone got mud on *his or her* face.

A little wordy, maybe, but at least it's clear and accurate. And why not really mix it up with *her or his?*

Everyone got mud on *her/his* face.

The slash has arrived. If you like *her/his*, you'll love *s/he!*

Everyone got mud on *her* face.

The shoe's on the other foot now, with the feminine pronoun *her* used to refer to everyone including men. Deal with it guys!

Everyone got mud on *their* face.

Flout the rule (yes, I said "flout," not "flaunt," and I should know which is which; I've done plenty of both in my day!) that says you can't use the plural pronoun *their* with the singular antecedent *everyone*. Heck, at least it sounds about right.

All the people got mud on their faces.

As a last resort, find a different indefinite pronoun!

For Whom the Pronoun Tolls

The problem of pronoun case is a familiar grammar accident just waiting to happen. To whom does it happen? To me, to you, to just about everyone, that's to whom!

As you may remember from Chapter 2, English grammar is sensitive to the distinctions among things that do things (subjects), things otherwise involved in the doing (objects), and things that get things done to them (indirect objects). Although nouns have subject and object cases, the distinction doesn't show up in the forms (inflections) of nouns. But it does show up in the forms (inflections) of pronouns.

> ### Grammar Jammer
>
> Think English is a nuisance because it has three cases for pronouns? Just be glad you're not studying Latin grammar, which has six cases for nouns as well as pronouns! An older language, proto-Indo European, has eight case forms: nominative (subject), genitive (possessive), dative, associative-instrumental, ablative, accusative, locative, and vocative.

Take a look at this sentence:

I love her when she does that.

Notice the two pronouns *her* and *she*. Both have the same implied antecedent—some female who does something in a lovable way. Let's say the antecedent is a dog named Goober. If we replace the pronouns with their antecedent, the sentence becomes ...

I love Goober when Goober does that.

Again, the two pronouns in the original sentence, *her* and *she*, both refer to Goober. The pronouns are different, though, because one takes the subject case (*she*) and the other takes the object case (*her*). *Goober* is an object (*her*) when it receives the action of the verb *love. Goober* is the subject when it performs the action of the verb *does.*

You could probably tell that the following sentence is incorrect, even if it weren't labeled:

> *Incorrect:* I love she when her does that.

Most people can hear the incorrect use of most pronouns, rather like a wrong note in music. But some instances often trip people up. Can you tell that all the following sentences are also incorrect:

1. *Incorrect:* It's me.
   Correct: It's I.

2. *Incorrect:* The culprit was him.
   Correct: The culprit was he.

3. *Incorrect:* Who are you talking about?
   Correct: Whom are you talking about?

Margin of Error

An owl that says "whooom" isn't necessarily any wiser than one that says "whooo." The smartest owls know when to say "who" and "whom"!

4. *Incorrect:* I'm always hungrier than her.
   Correct: I'm always hungrier than she.

5. *Incorrect:* Santa gave a present to Stacy and I.
   Correct: Santa gave a present to Stacy and me.

6. *Incorrect:* The gardener gave we three bikers a lecture.
   Correct: The gardener gave us three bikers a lecture.
7. *Incorrect:* Flora and me installed the new software.
   Correct: Flora and I installed the new software.

Kind of tricky, isn't it? Some of the correct sentences may even sound funny to you. "Whom are you talking about?" "It's I." Are people really supposed to talk this way? In fact, hardly anyone does. But it's nice to be able to, so the following section presents some hints to help you decide whether to use subject pronouns or object pronouns under tricky circumstances.

Casing the Joint

Ordinarily, most people have a gut feeling for when to use subject and object pronouns, but certain sentences, such as those in the preceding list, tend to cross them up. Such tricky sentences include those with compound subjects or objects and those in which the subject comes after the object.

Then there's the vexed question of whether the pronoun comes after a conjunction (words such as *and*, *or*, and *but* that connect other words to one another) or a preposition (words such as *for*, *to*, and *about* that link objects to other words in the sentence). You can read about both conjunctions and prepositions in Chapter 6.

Look again at the preceding list of sample sentences. Sentences 1 through 3 have subjects that are placed after the object. Sentence 4 makes a comparison. Sentences 5 and 6 have compound objects. Sentence 7 has a compound subject.

Which Comes First?

First let's think about those sentences that have an object that comes before the subject. Sentences such as these are actually much less common than sentences in which the subject comes first. In fact, the order of words in a sentence often indicates which nouns are used as subjects and which are used as objects—and sometimes greatly changes the meaning. Compare these two sentences:

Tom ate a shark.

A shark ate Tom.

In the first sentence, *Tom* is the subject and *shark* is the object; vice versa in the second sentence. This is consistent with the tendency in English to put the subject before the verb and the object afterward. But as we've seen, exceptions occur.

If you're not sure whether a pronoun is supposed to be a subject or an object, playing around with the order of words in the sentence can help you figure it out. The following three sentences can be changed so the subjects fall at the beginning without changing their meanings:

I am it. (*I* is the subject.)

He was the culprit. (*He* is the subject.)

You are talking about whom? (*Whom* is the object.)

When the sentences are re-stated so the subjects come first, it's often easier to identify the subjects and the objects.

Compounding the Problem

Sentences that have compound subjects or objects can also be tricky. It's pretty easy to figure them out, though, simply by restating the sentence without compound construction. See what happens when you change the sentence "Santa gave the present to Stacy and me." to "Santa gave the present to me." It's easier to tell that *me*, the object case pronoun, is correct.

Conversely, when you restate the sentence "Flora and I installed the new software." to "I installed the new software." it becomes pretty clear that *I* is a subject.

Invidious Comparisons

Sentences that draw comparisons or make contrasts between two things can also be tricky, because the terms of contrast or comparison are typically stated only once, even though they are grammatically related to two or more things. Consider, for example, the following sentence:

I am always hungrier than she.

This can be considered a compact, economical way of saying, "I am always hungrier than she is hungry." When you see that the pronoun *she* could be stated as part of the phrase "she is hungry," it's clear that *she*, the subject case pronoun, is correct. When you link the terms of comparison to both things being compared, it's often easier to tell whether pronouns should be subjects or objects.

Here's another example: to restate the sentence "There's no one here but us." you could say "There's no one here, but we are here." Again, if you include the missing phrase, it becomes clear that *we*, the subject case pronoun, is correct.

But wait! There are actually two opposed camps on this issue. Some grammarians argue that the object case is correct. To understand this opposing argument, it helps to know something about the part of speech known as the preposition.

Prepositions You Can't Refuse

Prepositions are those little words that relate nouns or pronouns to other words in the sentence. *To, for, at, above,* and *through* are just a few of the many prepositions. A preposition usually comes before a noun or a pronoun, but sometimes comes afterward. A preposition together with its noun or pronoun makes up a prepositional phrase. The prepositional phrase modifies some other word in the sentence.

Here are some examples of prepositional phrases:

> Through the haze
>
> In my lifetime
>
> Around town
>
> At your convenience

In these examples, *through, in, around,* and *at* are prepositions. *Haze, lifetime, town,* and *convenience* are called objects of the preposition. When the object of the preposition is a pronoun, it always takes the objective case, as in this example:

> *Correct:* I thought about them all day

Here *them* is the object of the preposition *about.*

With me so far? Good. Now here's the tricky part. Some words can be considered either prepositions or conjunctions, namely *as, but* (used to mean except), and *than.* When a personal pronoun follows one of these words, it can take either the subject or object case. Take another look at these examples:

> I am always hungrier than she/her.
>
> There's no one here but we/us.

Previously I said that the subject case is correct because the pronouns *she* (first example) and *we* (second example) are the subjects of implied phrases (she is hungry, we are here). Arguably, however, I could say the pronouns in question are objects of the prepositions *than* and *but*, respectively. If so, the object case (than she, but us) is correct.

Reflex Mechanism

Some pronouns are reflexive, meaning they refer to nouns that perform an action on or for themselves. Reflexive pronouns are *myself, yourself, himself, herself, itself, ourselves, yourselves,* and *themselves. Theirselves* is an incorrect way to say *themselves.* Here's a sentence that contains a reflexive pronoun:

> Mr. Holland excused himself.

Here the reflexive pronoun, *himself,* has the same antecedent as the subject, *Mr. Holland.*

> **Grammar Jammer** _____
>
> Another useful way to categorize pronouns is by person. First-person pronouns are *I, me, we,* and *us.* The second-person pronoun is *you.* Third-person pronouns include *she, he, it,* and *they.* Some critics say not to use the first person in formal expository writing. Not me. I say, go for it.

Reflexive pronouns are sometimes used for emphasis and to exclude other possible subjects. In the sentence "She did it herself." the reflexive pronoun *herself* doesn't receive the action of the verb, *did,* but emphasizes the subject, *she,* and indicates that *she* acted alone.

Reflexive pronouns sometimes get misused by people who want to sound formal. Check out this sentence:

> The company placed complete trust in myself.

I guess this is supposed to be kind of official sounding, but if you talk like this too much, people like me will laugh at you. And then myself will make jokes about how important yourself must think you are to be making ordinary personal pronouns reflexive all the time. But that's just myself.

The Least You Need to Know

- All pronouns must refer to nouns, whether implied or stated, called antecedents.
- Pronouns can be personal, demonstrative, relative, interrogative, or indefinite.
- The masculine pronoun *he* is no longer widely accepted in referring to groups that may include women. Instead, use an alternative such as *she or he*.
- Pronouns are inflected for subject case, object case, and possessive case.
- Reflexive pronouns refer to nouns that perform an action on themselves.

Where the Action Is: Verbs

In This Chapter

- ◆ Verbs: linking, transitive, helper—and more!
- ◆ All tensed up: present, past, and future for simple, progressive, perfect, and perfect progressive
- ◆ Fun with verbals: infinitives, gerunds, participles
- ◆ Active and passive voice
- ◆ Moods: indicative, imperative, subjunctive

Ever take a long-coveted new toy or tool out of the box; admire its smart, sleek design and useful features; flip on the switch; and ... nothing? Then the problem becomes clear: batteries not included!

Gizmos need batteries to function. Well, sentences are kind of like gizmos. They need verbs, which are kind of like the batteries of sentences. Without verbs, sentences don't work. In fact, you can't really even call it a sentence if there's no verb in it.

Verbs, like batteries, come in all different shapes and sizes. You need to be sure you have the right one that fits the sentence properly and delivers the right amount of juice in the right way. So strap on your grammatical volt meter, and let's see if we can get a charge out of the English language's most energizing part of speech.

Acting the Part with Verbs

As you may remember from grade school, verbs are the part of speech that represents action, so whenever there's action going on, you need verbs to tell about it. Verbs are so important in grammar that you can't build a sentence without including at least one. For example, "Go." is a complete sentence consisting of a single verb. "Pancake." in contrast, is not a complete sentence if you're talking about the breakfast food, which is a noun. If, however, you're using the word *pancake* as a verb, then it *is* a complete sentence. For example, if you want to tell a wrestler what move to execute on his opponent, you can say "Pancake!" as in, "Pancake that guy right on his back!"

Grammar Jammer

One indication of the basic importance of verbs to the language is the fact that the word *verb* comes from the Latin word *verbum,* which means "word." The English words *verbiage, verbose,* and *verbalize* all refer to words in general rather than to verbs specifically.

Of course, most sentences have both nouns and verbs, but the point is, verbs are essential to our language. Without verbs, the nouns and pronouns in our sentences wouldn't have anything to do. They couldn't even exist, because simply being is an action that can be expressed only with a verb.

Verbs are all about action, but the form they take depends on the noun or pronoun that performs the action and on when and how the action takes place. Verbs can change form depending on whether the action takes place in the past, present, or future and depending on who or what acts. They even change form depending on whether the action happens, might happen, or is commanded to happen.

Inflectious Enthusiasm

Grammarians love to inflect verbs. They even have a special word (a verb, in fact) for what they do when they inflect verbs: *conjugate*. (No, not *that* kind of conjugation! "Grammarians do it with verbs"—how's that for a bumper sticker?) Conjugating verbs is a time-honored way to study the basics of grammar, especially when you're studying a foreign language.

Parse Words _____

Conjugation is the practice of inflecting verbs for person and tense. It's good practice for language students.

Let's do a little conjugating now. Here's the verb *to boogie*, inflected for the simple present tense and to agree with the different personal pronouns:

> I boogie.
>
> You boogie.
>
> He/she/it boogies.
>
> We boogie.
>
> They boogie.

For some extra fun, you can conjugate a few verbs on your own. You'll see that the verb form is usually the same for all the pronouns except for he/she/it, which usually has an added *s* at the end. Grammar does have some patterns.

Getting Tense

Verb inflections that show past, present, or future action are called *tenses*. In addition, each of the tenses has four different tenses: *simple, progressive, perfect,* and *perfect progressive:* 'Scuse me while I conjugate!

	Past	**Present**	**Future**
Simple	We boogied.	We boogie.	We will boogie.
Progressive	We were boogieing.	We are boogieing.	We will be boogieing.
Perfect	We had boogied.	We have boogied.	We will have boogied.
Perfect progressive	We had been boogieing.	We have been boogieing.	We will have been boogieing

See how rich life can be when you know how to boogie in the future perfect progressive tense?

This Is Highly Irregular

There's a pattern in the way verbs inflect for tense as well as for person (to agree with the personal pronouns). But with tenses, the pattern isn't rigid. Some verbs, called *irregular verbs*, do things a little differently from the others. Non-native speakers and little kids just learning English get tripped up on irregular verbs all the time.

To eat is an irregular verb. The simple past tense isn't *eated*; it's *ate*. English has hundreds of irregular verbs that we have to learn by ear, one at a time.

Grammar Jammer

Studies of language acquisition in small children show that, before they sense a pattern behind verb inflections, children learn to use verbs correctly by imitating older speakers. Then, after coming to see the pattern, they apply it too rigidly and make mistakes they didn't make before when using irregular verbs.

Irregularity crops up with the simple past tense form of verbs but also with what is known as the past participle, which I discuss more later in this chapter, in the section on verbals. Usually, the past participle is the same as the simple past tense, as in the verb *to hurry*, for which the simple past tense and the past participle are both *hurried.* The past participle of the verb *to eat* is *eaten,* another irregular form.

You'll encounter plenty of irregular past participles. Even native speakers sometimes stumble on some of them. In addition, a few have nonstandard regional variants.

Back to Basics: Predicates

You know by now that verbs are necessary parts of complete sentences. To be complete, a sentence needs a subject, which is a noun, and a *predicate,* which includes a verb. A predicate is the part of the sentence that defines the action carried out by the subject. The predicate may include any word or phrase that modifies the verb, together with the object of the sentence, but it always must include a verb.

Parse Words

A **predicate** is the part of a sentence that defines the subject. It includes the verb and may also include any words or phrases modifying the verb as well as the object of the sentence.

Changing the Subject

The relationship between the subject and its predicate is called *predication.* A common grammar problem to avoid is faulty predication, or when there's an improper, illogical relationship between the subject and predicate. The best way to tell whether predication is faulty is to look at the noun and see if it makes sense as the subject of the predicate.

Here's an example of faulty predication:

> *Incorrect:* My belief in Clement turned out to be a big disappointment.

Although *belief* is the subject of this sentence, the predicate actually describes Clement. The sentence should be revised to the following:

> *Correct:* I believed in Clement, but he turned out to be a big disappointment.

Here's another sentence with faulty predication:

> *Incorrect:* The directions to the school go on for another 3 miles.

 Margin of Error

It's always faulty predication to say "the reason is because ..." as in the sentence "The reason I came back is because I got lost." The sentence should be changed to say either "I came back because I got lost." or "The reason I came back is *that* I got lost."

This sentence says the *directions* go on for 3 miles. It should say this:

> *Correct:* The road indicated by the directions goes on for 3 miles.

Missing Links

Many sentences with faulty predication include *linking verbs*. These verbs relate the subject of a sentence to the subject complement, suggesting the subject and subject complement are similar or equivalent. (You can find subjects and complements discussed in Chapter 2.) In other words, linking verbs work something like the way an equal sign (=) works in an equation. The most common linking verbs are *be, seem, appear, become, look, taste, feel,* and *sound.* Here are some linking verbs in action:

> *Correct:* I feel silly.

> *Correct:* Bread gets moldy.

> *Correct:* The moon looks reddish.

> *Correct:* Water is a precious resource.

Parse Words

Linking verbs relate the subject of a sentence to the subject complement, suggesting similarity or equivalence between the two.

If the linking verb links a subject with a complement that can't be considered an equivalent or similar thing, you have a case of faulty predication on your hands. Here are some examples of faulty predication:

Incorrect: The ad for pastry looks filling.

Incorrect: The time it takes to get ready is hard work.

Incorrect: Grilling food outdoors is a fun way to cook and also tastes great.

The linking verbs in the preceding sentences—*looks, is,* and *tastes,* respectively—are mistakenly used to link subjects with complements that don't work with them. They're not similar things. The sentences should be changed to read:

Correct: The pastry in the ad looks filling.

Correct: Getting ready takes time and is hard work.

Correct: Food grilled outdoors is fun to cook and also tastes great.

Verbs in Transit

If a verb is not a linking verb, it is either a *transitive* or an *intransitive verb.* Transitive verbs are those that require objects. (You may have read about objects in Chapter 2.) In the sentence "She wanted a sandwich." *wanted* is a transitive verb because it needs the object, *a sandwich,* to complete the predicate.

Parse Words _____

A **transitive verb** describes action that is carried out by the subject on an object. An **intransitive verb** doesn't take an object.

If the verb by itself leaves you hanging, expecting more information than it provides, it's a transitive verb. Take a look at the subject and verb, "They need." *Need* is a transitive verb because something is needed for the statement to make sense. That something is the object of the sentence. "They need fertilizer."

In contrast, intransitive verbs are those that don't require an object. In the sentence "We slept until noon." *slept* is an intransitive verb. *Until noon* is not an object, but a modifier that isn't structurally or logically necessary. *We slept* makes sense on its own, so *slept* is intransitive.

Many verbs can be used as both transitive and intransitive verbs. *To sleep* is usually intransitive, as in the preceding example, but it is transitive in this example:

He slept himself out of a job.

Here *slept* is transitive because it takes the object, *himself.* Of course, *slept* isn't usually used this way, but it makes perfect sense to say this about someone who got fired for napping at work.

Verbal Tea

When is a verb not a verb? When it's a *verbal.*
When verbs don't function as verbs, but as nouns,
adjectives, or adverbs, they're called verbals.
Verbals take one of three different forms:

- ♦ **Infinitive.** The verb form in which the base
  verb is preceded by *to,* as in "to inquire,"
  "to be," and "to climb."

- ♦ **Gerund (the present participle used as a
  noun).** The verb form in which *ing* is added
  to the base verb, as in *running, elaborating,*
  and *typing.*

- ♦ **Past participle.** The verb form ending in
  ed, such as *sniffed, asked,* and *expected.*

Parse Words _____

Verbals are verb forms that may be
used as nouns or adjectives. They include
infinitives, gerunds (present participles
used as nouns), and past participles.

Ready for some examples? Here's the gerund *sleep-
ing* used in a sentence as a noun:

> Sleeping is an art form that must be perfected
> through practice.

The same word can also be used as an adjective:

> It's wise to let sleeping artists lie.

Here's the infinitive, *to slip,* used as a noun:

> To slip while walking and chewing gum could be disastrous.

OK! **Grammar Rules, OK!**

Old-school grammarians say it's wrong to split infinitives, that is, to insert an adverb between the *to* and the main verbal. Here's a split infinitive:

> I like to always talk with my mouth full.

The infinitive, *to talk,* is split by the adverb *always.* According to traditional rules of grammar, this sentence is a no-no and should be corrected to read as follows:

> I always like to talk with my mouth full.

Can you think of a way to use the infinitive *to slip* as an adjective? How about this:

> I resist the temptation to slip while walking and chewing gum.

Here, *to slip* is used as an adjective modifying the noun *temptation.* In fact, *temptation* is the object of the sentence, while *to slip* is what's known as the *object complement.* (You can read about objects in Chapter 2 and about object complements in Chapter 5.)

Infinitives are used more frequently as nouns than as adjectives, but here's another example of an adjective infinitive, although I may be pushing the envelope here. See if you think the infinitive *to do* works when used as an adjective in this example:

> I have a lot on my to-do list.

It helps to put a hyphen between *to* and *do* to keep things clear. Infinitives, by the way, are not typically used with hyphens. (You can read about hyphens in Chapter 11. I'm not trying to bounce you around from chapter to chapter, but heck, grammar is such a rich tapestry it sometimes helps to see the different strands in context.)

Infinitives can also be used as adverbs, as in these examples:

> We hope to do well.
>
> Sandy went home to sleep.

In the first of these two sentences, the infinitive *to do* modifies the verb *hope*. In the second sentence, *to sleep* modifies the verb *went*.

Moving on, here's a past participle, *disgusted*, used as an adjective:

> The disgusted baker threw away the entire batch of cookies.

Strictly speaking, past participles don't get used as nouns, although they may be used as adjectives that stand for nouns. Permit me to explain: sometimes adjectives modify nouns that are implied but not stated. For example, in the adage "There's no rest for the weary." *weary* is an adjective modifying an unstated noun, *people.* You can use past participles in the same way:

> There's no rest for the disgusted.

Here's Help

Verbals can be used as nouns or adjectives, but they can also be used as verbs, provided they get help— *helping verbs,* in fact. Verbs may be single words or groups of words that include helping verbs, also called auxiliary verbs. Helping verbs are combined with the main verb to create the complete verb. We've already seen that helping verbs can be used to make the progressive, perfect, and perfect progressive tenses. In the verb phrase "will have been boogieing," *will, have,* and *been* are all helping verbs.

OK! **Grammar Rules, OK!** _____

Helping verbs are sometimes used for emphasis and to ask questions. For example, in the sentence "I did take out the laundry." *did* is a helping verb. In the sentence "Will you arrive on time?" *will* is a helping verb.

Helping verbs are also used to make the *passive voice.* In passive voice, as opposed to *active voice,* the subject of the sentence receives, rather than carries out, the action described by the verb. You could say that passive construction takes the object of a sentence and states it as the subject. Here's a famous example of passive voice:

A good time was had by all.

Contrast the same sentence changed to active voice:

All had a good time.

Margin of Error

Passive construction isn't incorrect, but overuse of the passive voice tends to make writing vague and flabby. Active voice is generally more clear and direct.

In writing, it's generally a good idea to avoid passive voice. In fact, some grammarians complain that the verb *to be* is overused even in the active voice and recommend using other, more meaningful and specific verbs instead.

A special group of helping verbs, called *modal verbs*, express degrees of ability, inclination, or obligation. They include *can, could, may, might, will, would, must, ought, shall,* and *should.* For example:

We might stay out all night.

We should do our homework.

We will be in trouble tomorrow.

In the Mood

Verbs correspond to person, have tenses, and have active or passive voice. Quick! Make up a sentence that uses the active voice, progressive tense, and third person. Give up? Here's one:

> The basket was heaped with walnuts.

No problem! So what else is there to know about verbs? The coolest thing of all: *verb mood*.

Parse Words

Verb mood indicates whether an action takes the form of a statement or question, a command, or a possibility. The three verb moods are indicative, imperative, and subjunctive.

Verbs come in three moods:

- **Indicative (also called declarative) mood** is the most common of the three, the standard mood to use when saying how things are. Such sentences as "Cows eat grass." and "The bank tellers wore ridiculous costumes." have verbs in the indicative mood.

- **Imperative mood** is the command form used when telling someone to do something. The base form of the verb is used and the subject (you) is usually implied rather than stated. "Go slowly." and "Please respond

by telephone." are sentences with verbs in the
imperative mood. So is "Pancake the guy
right on his back!"

♦ **Subjunctive mood** is the trickiest. It is used
when the action represented by the verb
might not really happen. "If I had time, I
would wash the car." Here, *had* and *would* are
both subjunctive. "Let's be friends." Here *be* is
subjunctive. "I should go back to the office."
Here *should* is subjunctive.

Grammar Jammer

It has become common practice among
many sportscasters to use the indicative
rather than the subjunctive mood to describe
hypothetical situations. For example, when
the shortstop on a baseball team makes a
costly error, the announcer might say, "If the
shortstop makes that play, it's a whole different game!" To restate the sentence properly,
"If the shortstop had made that play, it
would be a whole different game."

Subjunctive mood isn't used as extensively as it used
to be and failures to use it are increasing. Nevertheless, it's a good thing to know. "If I was ..." still
sounds unrefined and should be corrected to "if I
were ..." On the other hand, hardly anyone still says,
"If it should rain, our croquet match would be
ruined." Most people now are more comfortable

using the indicative mood and say, "If it rains, our match will be ruined."

The Least You Need to Know

- ◆ Verbs are inflected (change form) according to person, tense, and mood.
- ◆ Predication is the relation of the verb and its modifiers to the subject.
- ◆ Linking verbs relate subjects to the subject complements.
- ◆ Transitive verbs require an object; intransitive verbs do not.
- ◆ Infinitives and past and present participles make up verbal phrases that can be used as nouns or adjectives.
- ◆ The three verb moods are indicative, imperative, and subjunctive.

Totally Mod: Modifiers

In This Chapter

- ◆ Adjectives and adverbs
- ◆ Positive, comparative, and superlative forms
- ◆ Adverbial and adjectival phrases
- ◆ Misplaced, squinting, and dangling modifiers

Modifiers are great for larding sentences with layers of meaning, interesting detail, color, and specificity. They describe, define, qualify, and characterize. They enliven, enlarge, illuminate, and illustrate. But as with any other part of speech, the benefits are fraught with grammatical peril.

This chapter is about adverbs and adjectives, the phrases they make up, and the parts of speech they modify. It's also about the various things that go wrong when they're used incorrectly.

A Few Modifications

Modifiers are words and phrases that describe or qualify other words and phrases. Modifiers include adjectives and adverbs. They can be single words or adjectival or adverbial phrases. The words and phrases they modify include nouns, pronouns, verbs, and other adjectives and adverbs. More specifically, adjectives modify nouns and pronouns; adverbs modify verbs, adjectives, and other adverbs.

Margin of Error

Adjectives should not be used to modify verbs, although it's a common mistake. It's improper to say, "move quick," "do it good," and "talk nice." The correct things to say are "move quickly," "do it well," and "talk nicely."

The Cutting Adj.

Adjectives include words such as *dirty, bold, green, hungry, graceful,* and *obtuse.* They can appear before the noun or pronoun they modify, or as the subject complement, separated from the word they modify by a linking verb.

The house was green.

The green house was recently painted.

Here the adjective, *green*, appears first as the complement to the subject, *house*, and second as an ordinary modifier.

Many adjectives can be formed by adding *ed* to the end of a verb. This is called the past participle of the verb, as you may have read in Chapter 4. *Dilapidated, spoken,* and *handled* are all past participles and can be used as adjectives, as in *dilapidated car, spoken word,* and *groomed iguana.*

How-To with Adverbs

You can think of adverbs as how-to words, because they explain how actions take place. Adverbs include words such as *happily, smoothly, fast,* and *squarely* and can modify adjectives and other adverbs, as well as verbs.

Margin of Error

Lots of people say "sure" when they're asked to do something. Strictly speaking, this is incorrect, because doing something is a verb. The proper response is the adverb, "surely."

Here are some adverbs in action:

> He sneezed loudly.
>
> The duck busily waddled.
>
> The cow was amazingly purple.

Here *loudly* modifies the verb *sneezed, busily* modifies the verb *waddled,* and *amazingly* modifies the adjective *purple.* Notice that adverbs can be placed before or after the words they modify.

Typically, you can make an adverb by adding *ly* to the end of an adjective. In fact, it's a common mistake to use an adjective (without the *ly*) to modify a verb. In these sentences, adjectives are mistakenly used to modify verbs:

> *Incorrect:* Carmen sings good.
>
> *Incorrect:* Always try to speak correct.
>
> *Incorrect:* He answered quick.

These sentences should be corrected as follows:

> *Correct:* Carmen sings well.
>
> *Correct:* Always try to speak correctly.
>
> *Correct:* He answered quickly.

❗ Grammar Jammer

Adverbs are the words that usually end in *ly*. However, not all adverbs end in *ly*, including *fast, well*, and *very*. What's more, some words that end in *ly* aren't adverbs, including *wily, timely, elderly*, and *folly*.

Notice that *well* is the adverbial form of the adjective *good*. In fact, *good* is frequently misused as an adverb. When someone asks how you're doing, the grammatically correct response is *well:*

> I'm doing well.
>
> You look well.
>
> They performed well.

Other adjectives frequently misused as adverbs are *bad*, *real*, and *sure:*

> *Incorrect:* You sure eat a lot.
>
> *Incorrect:* You must be real hungry.
>
> *Incorrect:* You seem to crave food awful bad.

These sentences should·be corrected to read as follows:

> *Correct:* You surely eat a lot.
>
> *Correct:* You must be really hungry.
>
> *Correct:* You seem to crave food awfully badly.

Compare This

Adjectives and adverbs take three different forms, two of which are used when making comparisons:

- ♦ **Positive form** is the base form of adjectives and adverbs. It is not used for comparisons. Examples include rough and roughly.
- ♦ **Comparative form** is used to compare two things. It's formed by adding *er* to the end of the base form or by putting *more* or *less* before it. Examples include *rougher* and *more roughly.*
- ♦ **Superlative form** is used to compare three or more things. It's formed by adding *est* to the end of the base form or by using the words *most* and *least* in front of it. Examples include *most rough* and *most roughly.*

More or Less, Most or Least?

Many adjectives and adverbs don't take the *er* and *est* endings, such as *ridiculous* and *ridiculously*. For these words, adding *more, less, most,* or *least,* makes the comparative and superlative forms, as in the sentence "Try to be the least ridiculous of all the performers."

Margin of Error

The adjectives *less* and *fewer* are often confused. *Less* should be used with noncount nouns; *fewer* should be used with count nouns:

We've had less rain this year than last year, and there are fewer leaves on the trees.

Some adjectives and adverbs have irregular comparative and superlative forms. For example, *good, better, best* and *bad, worse, worst.* The positive modifiers *some, much,* and *many* all have the same comparative form, namely *more,* and the same superlative form, to wit, *most.*

Beyond Compare

Certain problems commonly crop up when using comparative and superlative forms. One is the double comparison, which is improper and results in comparison overkill. Statements such as "more flatter" and "most prettiest" are incorrect.

A more subtle difficulty in using the comparative forms is in making certain that things are fully compared. Here's a lazy comparison, followed by its proper comparison:

> *Incorrect:* People with certain skin conditions experience more discomfort than allergies.

> *Correct:* People with certain skin conditions experience more discomfort than people with allergies.

Here's another lazy comparison, along with its corrected form:

> *Incorrect:* My dog has a bigger nose than Barry's Chihuahua.

> *Correct:* My dog has a bigger nose than that of Barry's Chihuahua.

Grammar Jammer

Some adjectives have been used without the nouns they modify for so long, they practically seem to have become nouns in their own right. How about *bubbly* (for champagne)? And I bet you don't know what noun the adjective phrase "the light fantastic" originally modified. The phrase was used without a noun in the old 1890's song that goes "We'll trip the light fantastic on the sidewalks of New York." It was used originally, however, by the seventeenth-century British poet, John Milton, who said "Come, and trip it as ye go / Upon the light fantastic toe." *Toe* is the missing noun. So to "trip the light fantastic" means to dance on your toes.

In a Phrase

Ready to get fancy with modifiers? Modifiers include
entire phrases and clauses as well as individual adjectives and adverbs. These may be verbal phrases (with
verbs used as modifiers), prepositional phrases,
appositive phrases, or absolute phrases.

Verbals Revisited

Verbal phrases are modifiers made out of verb forms
called verbals (see Chapter 4 for a verbal refresher).
Verbal phrases include present participial phrases,
past participial phrases, and infinitive phrases.

Consider these examples:

> The politician did all he could to keep his extra-
> marital affairs a secret.

Here, the infinitive phrase "to keep his extramarital
affairs a secret" is used as an adverb to modify the
verb phrase "did all he could."

> Swimming for my life, I didn't have time to
> wonder how I had fallen in the water.

"Swimming for my life" is a present participial phrase
used as an adjective modifying the subject, "I."

> Thinking about the horror movie, Ormond
> found it impossible to sleep.

Here, "thinking about the horror movie" is a present
participial phrase used as an adjective to modify the
subject, "Sandy."

> We wandered through the construction site, which
> was littered with debris.

In this example, "littered with debris" is a past participial phrase used as an adjective to modify the object "construction site."

> Morris awoke twisted up in the sheets.

Here, "twisted up in the sheets" is a past participial phrase used as an adverb to modify the verb, "awoke."

Absolute Modifier

A special kind of participial phrase is the *absolute phrase*. An absolute phrase is a modifier made from a verbal phrase that modifies everything else in the sentence:

> The guest speaker having departed early, the
> history club was left to its usual business.

Here the absolute phrase, "The guest speaker having departed early," modifies the rest of the sentence.

Absolute phrases can lend a sophisticated tone to a piece of writing and provide a good way to weed out unnecessary conjunctions such as *and*. Sometimes, however, they are overused, especially when they don't contain much information. Absolute phrases based on the verb "to be," for example, often lack meaning:

> That being the case ...
>
> All things being equal ...
>
> Be it as it may ...

Prepped to Modify

Prepositional phrases are phrases that begin with prepositions—words such as *at, to, with,* and *about*. (You can read about prepositions in Chapter 6.) Prepositions relate transitive verbs to their objects. (You can read about transitive verbs in Chapter 4.) A prepositional phrase includes a preposition and its object and typically functions as an adjective or adverb:

> Uncle Ed likes to go driving on Sundays with his pet ferret.

Here, "on Sundays" and "with his pet ferret" are both prepositional phrases used as adverbs modifying the verb "go driving."

Accentuate Appositive

Appositive phrases are adjectival phrases that explain or identify nouns. They occur directly after the nouns they modify. They aren't grammatically necessary to the sentences they belong to, but they do serve nicely as mid-sentence definitions of key words, set apart by commas:

> Squash, a fast-moving indoor racquet sport, is rising in popularity among college students.

Here the appositive phrase "a fast-moving indoor racquet sport" modifies the noun "squash."

> **Grammar Jammer** _____
>
> The famous song "Doe, a Deer" from
> _The Sound of Music_ is made up almost
> completely of appositive phrases, together
> with the nouns they modify—_do, re, mi,
> fa, so, la, ti,_ and _do._

Let Me Rephrase That

Special challenges arise when using phrases as modifiers. Adjectival and adverbial phrases can really load sentences with information, supplying extra significance, tying loose strands together, and clearing up areas of doubt. But if those phrases aren't well placed, things can get ugly and confusing. Fortunately, grammarians have phrase problems all figured out.

Three different mistakes crop up from time to time with modifying phrases: misplaced modifiers, dangling modifiers, and squinting modifiers.

Out of Place

In general, modifiers should be placed as closely as possible to the words they modify. Putting them somewhere else often results in _misplaced modifiers_. Misplaced modifiers are modifying phrases that occur in inopportune places in a sentence, making it unclear which word they are intended to modify:

I got a job yesterday with a company installing computers.

Here the modifier "installing computers" is misplaced. It should be placed after the noun it modifies: "job."

Don't Look Now

A special kind of misplaced modifier is the *squinting modifier*. A squinting modifier occurs (confusingly) between two words, either of which it might modify:

> The mission Scooter completed just barely earned him his promotion.

Here the modifier "just barely" could be taken to modify either "completed" or "earned him his promotion." The sentence should be changed to read as either of the following:

> The mission Scooter just barely completed earned him his promotion.

> The mission Scooter completed earned him his promotion—just barely.

Left Dangling

Whenever you use a modifier, it's important to include the word to be modified! When you don't, you get a *dangling modifier*. These phrases mistakenly modify words not actually in the sentence:

> *Incorrect:* Muscles aching, aerobics class seemed to go on forever.

Here, "muscles aching" is intended to modify a noun that isn't included in the sentence.

> *Incorrect:* Finally protected with lots of sun block, a thick bank of clouds rolled in.

Here again, the modifier "Finally protected with lots of sun block" has nothing to modify.

Don't confuse dangling modifiers with absolute phrases. Absolute phrases have their own subject, whereas dangling modifiers need a subject that isn't provided. In addition, absolute phrases modify not just one word, but an entire sentence. Dangling modifiers are intended to modify a single, unstated word.

The Least You Need to Know

- ◆ Adjectives modify nouns; adverbs modify verbs, adjectives, and other adverbs.

- ◆ Modifiers can take positive, comparative, and superlative forms. Comparative and superlative forms are used in making comparisons.

- ◆ An absolute phrase is a modifier made from a verbal phrase that modifies a whole sentence.

- ◆ An appositive phrase is an adjectival phrase that explains or identifies a noun.

- ◆ Misplaced modifiers, squinting modifiers, and dangling modifiers are common problems that arise when using phrases as modifiers.

Chapter **6**

Bits and Pieces

In This Chapter

- ◈ Articles
- ◈ Prepositions
- ◈ Conjunctions
- ◈ Interjections

Not all parts of speech are equally important. I've discussed some of the more important ones in previous chapters, so in this chapter let's talk about some of the less significant ones. But don't think these minor parts of speech—articles, prepositions, conjunctions, and interjections—don't deserve your time. They are well worth knowing about, especially because it can be easy to get mixed up when using some of these little words!

Many of these parts of speech, including articles and prepositions, serve mainly to pave the way for other words. Others, such as conjunctions, serve to link parts of speech together in various ways.

Interjections? Well, shoot! If a part of speech can be anything at all and nothing in particular, it's got to be an interjection.

Noun Determination

Inquiring minds want to know: can words belonging to different parts of speech serve similar functions? Yes! Pronouns, adjectives, and articles can all be *noun determiners*. A noun determiner is a word that lets you know a noun is coming next and tells something about what sort of noun it is.

> **Parse Words** _____
>
> **Noun determiners** are words that indicate that a noun must follow. Articles and some pronouns and adjectives can be noun determiners, as can cardinal numbers.

Pronouns Paving the Way

Many noun determiners are pronouns, including the demonstrative pronouns *this, that, these,* and *those,* and the possessive pronouns *my, your, her, its, their,* and *our.* Some adjectives are noun determiners, including *some, each, every, any, all,* and *another.* The cardinal numbers, *one, two, three,* and so on, can also be noun determiners.

You can see for yourself what noun determiners do for a noun just by picking one of them and saying it after each of these noun determiners in turn (that boy, every boy, our boy, one boy). They don't convey qualities pertaining to the noun itself, such as *red, scaly, fetid,* or *clammy.* Instead, they indicate something about how the noun fits in with its context.

Hot Articles

But wait! Notwithstanding the grammatical richness of the words I've just described, the panoply of noun determiners has not been exhausted. In fact, the classic noun determiners are the articles, *a, an,* and *the.*

Articles constitute one of the parts of speech all to themselves, even though there are only three of them. Nevertheless, these three words are divided into two grammatical categories: the *definite article* (*the*) and the *indefinite articles* (*a* and *an*).

> **Parse Words**
>
> The **definite article** (there's only one, the word *the*) is a noun determiner that points to a noun that has been introduced already or the specificity of which is understood. The **indefinite articles** (*a* and *an*) are noun determiners used to introduce nonspecific nouns.

The indefinite articles *a* and *an* are used with nouns that are introduced for the first time. "A ball," for example, could be any ball. The article *an* is used specifically to introduce nouns beginning with a vowel or vowel sound. "An orange" or "an hour" could be any orange or any hour.

Grammar Jammer

It used to be that the article *an* was used before words beginning with *h* that have an unaccented first syllable, as in "an humongous mistake." This rule has become obsolete.

The definite article *the* signifies that the noun it introduces is specific or, as the name indicates, definite. It is used to refer to nouns that have already been pointed out. "The ball" is a specific ball that has already been mentioned or whose existence as a specific thing is already understood.

Note the difference in the use of the indefinite and the definite article in the following sentence:

> When offered *a* bright red ball or *a* banana, Lulu, *the* chimp, chose *the* banana.

The indefinite article *a* introduces the nouns *ball* and *banana*. The definite article *the* refers to the noun *chimp*, whose specificity is understood, and to the noun *banana*, which was already introduced.

Well Prepped

There's a whole slew of little words known as *prepositions* that do the job of relating nouns to other nouns, pronouns, or verbs by turning them into modifiers called prepositional phrases. A prepositional phrase includes a preposition followed by a noun, called the object of the preposition.

Prepositions include the words *at, about, for, with, from, to, of,* and *around.*

Here's a sentence with a prepositional phrase used to modify a verb:

> The tarp protected the logs from rain and snow.

Here the preposition *from* relates the objects *rain and snow* to the verb *protected.* In other words, *from rain and snow* is a prepositional phrase that functions as an adverb modifying *protected.*

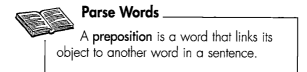

Parse Words

A **preposition** is a word that links its object to another word in a sentence.

People who spend their time counting things say there are about 150 different prepositions. Which ones get used when depends on their meaning and the meaning of the noun or pronoun they come before. Prepositions are idiomatic, so the only way to be certain you're using them properly is to check a dictionary.

Two commonly confused prepositions are *as* and *like. As* means "serving the purpose of," while *like* means "similar to." Strictly speaking, *like* should not be used to mean "serving the purpose of," although it is often used this way in colloquial or casual speech:

> *Incorrect:* Act like a grownup.
>
> *Correct:* Act as a grownup.

In formal speech and writing, *like* should not be used here, because it doesn't make much sense to tell someone who is already an adult to act similarly to herself. *Like* is proper, however, when making a comparison, as in this sentence:

> *Correct:* Run like a deer.

OK! **Grammar Rules, OK!** _____

Old-school grammarians say it's wrong to end a sentence with a preposition, but today most people think it's okay to do so. It used to be considered wrong to say "What did you do that for?" instead of "For what (or why) did you do that?"

Holding Things Together

Words that join parts of sentences are known as *conjunctions*. Conjunctions not only join words, phrases, and clauses, but they also indicate something about their logical relationship. There are two major kinds of conjunctions: *coordinating* and *subordinating*. Coordinating conjunctions include a special kind called *correlative conjunctions*.

Coordinates

Coordinating conjunctions join parts of a sentence that are grammatically similar to one another: nouns with nouns, verbs with verbs, phrases with phrases, and clauses with clauses. The coordinating

conjunctions include *and, but, or, nor, yet, for,* and *so.*
They are always placed between the parts they join.
Here are some coordinating conjunctions at work:

> Donated items may be new or slightly used.

> Ed likes cooking and going to the market.

Parse Words

Conjunctions are words that relate parts of a sentence to one another. **Coordinating conjunctions** relate parts that are grammatically similar. These include **correlative conjunctions,** which function in pairs. **Subordinating conjunctions** relate parts that are grammatically dissimilar.

When coordinating conjunctions join two independent clauses, a comma should appear before the conjunction, as in these examples:

> I have my credit card, but I don't have my checkbook.

> I can't have dairy products, so I eat a lot of tofu.

Traditional grammarians say one should never begin a sentence with a coordinating conjunction such as *and* or *but* because the purpose of such words is to link words within sentences. But there are many who believe that such rules were made to be broken!

Correlates

The correlative conjunction is a special kind of coordinating conjunction. Correlative conjunctions join grammatically similar parts of sentences just as ordinary coordinating conjunctions do, but they require two words, rather than just one, to do so. Correlative conjunctions include *as ... as, both ... and, either ... or, neither ... nor, not ... but,* and *whether ... or.*

Margin of Error

So and *such* are coordinating conjunctions that are often used for emphasis rather than to join parts of a sentence, as in ...

That meeting was *so* boring.

The chairperson is *such* a windbag.

Such usage is fine for casual speech but, strictly speaking, is incorrect, because the conjunctions need a second clause to join with the first:

That meeting was so boring I thought I had wandered into a Petrified Forest convention.

The chairperson is such a windbag it's a wonder that she doesn't float away on her own hot air.

Consider these examples:

Either finish your homework or go to bed.

Here, the two clauses "finish your homework" and "go to bed" are joined by the correlative conjunction "either ... or."

> You'll like this musical group whether or not you like to polka.

Here the two clauses, "you'll like this musical group" and "you like to polka" are joined by the correlative conjunction "whether ... or."

Subordinates

While coordinates are important, most conjunctions are subordinating, such as *after, although, as, because, before, how, if, once, since, than, that, though, till, until, when, where, whether,* and *while.* Subordinating conjunctions join dependent clauses to the main clause of a sentence. They are always placed before the dependent clause. (You can read about clauses in Chapter 7. For now, keep in mind that a clause contains a subject and a verb and that a sentence is made up of one or more clauses.) See if you can identify the subordinating conjunctions in the following sentences:

> You can't be a lifeguard until you get certified.
>
> If the flies bother you, you can work in the living room.
>
> While Susan slept, her dog ripped up her new photo album.

How'd you do? The subordinating conjunction in the first sentence is *until.* In the second sentence, it's *if*, and in the third sentence it's *while*. Notice that subordinating conjunctions introduce clauses that would make incomplete sentences if the clauses were removed and left standing alone.

> **OK!** **Grammar Rules, OK!**
> You can always tell a dependent clause from an independent clause by the subordinating conjunction that occurs before it.

Adverbial Hookup

Sometimes certain adverbs are used as conjunctions. Such adverbs are called *conjunctive adverbs*, and they join two independent clauses. They include *also, anyway, besides, consequently, finally, incidentally, meanwhile, moreover, nevertheless, otherwise, however,* and *therefore*.

Here are some conjunctive adverbs in action:

> I've never smelted iron before; however, I'll give it a try.

Notice the semicolon before the conjunctive adverb *however*. To link clauses properly, conjunctive adverbs require semicolons. Some require a comma afterward; others do not:

> It's a good idea to be careful; otherwise, you could hurt yourself.

Read more about semicolons in Chapter 9.

If I Might Interject ...

Interjections include some of the saltiest and most colorful phrases, as well as some of the most meaningless utterances people can make. Curses, expressions of surprise, and inadvertent or habitual sounds people make when speaking are all interjections. In formal speech and writing, interjections contribute virtually nothing and are usually unnecessary; however, it's hard to avoid using them in ordinary speech.

> **Parse Words**
>
> Interjections are words, phrases, or sounds inserted as exclamations.

Interjections can occur anywhere. They can occur within a sentence or form complete sentences on their own. They can even occur in the middle of a word. Interjections include sounds such as *hmmm,* *uhhh, oh!* and *shhh,* as well as *oh boy! yippie!* and *shucks!* And of course there are expressions like, "Well, I'll be a son of a mangy pole cat!"

Interjections are often curses or euphemistic variants of curses. In fact, there's a rich variety of interjections that seem intended to substitute for blasphemous curses. After all, religious people say it's wrong to use God's name in vain, so instead people say things like "Gee Whiz!" "Jeesum Crow!" "Cheese and Crackers!" "Gosh!" "Golly!" and "Jiminy Cricket!"

> ### Grammar Jammer _____
>
> You've probably heard the expression "expletive deleted," meaning that a blasphemous or obscene interjection has been censored. In fact, the word *expletive* can be used to mean "interjection." It also refers to terms that are inserted into a sentence for rhythmic or syntactical reasons, such as the word *it* in the sentence "It looks like rain," or the word *there* in the sentence, "There seems to be a problem."

The Least You Need to Know

- Noun determiners indicate that a noun is to follow, and include the indefinite articles *a* and *an* and the definite article *the*.

- A preposition is a word that links its object to other parts of the sentence.

- Conjunctions are words that relate parts of a sentence to one another. Coordinating conjunctions relate parts that are grammatically similar. Subordinating conjunctions relate parts that are grammatically dissimilar.

- Interjections are sounds, words, phrases, or whole sentences inserted as exclamations.

Putting the Parts Together

In This Chapter

- ♦ Phrases
- ♦ Clauses: dependent, independent, essential, and nonessential
- ♦ Coordination and subordination
- ♦ Sentences and fragments

As you may already be aware, the parts of speech can be combined into meaningful packages of various sizes, including phrases, clauses, and sentences. Phrases, clauses, and sentences, in turn, can be combined into larger, more meaningful packages. Assembling the parts well is essential to good grammar and makes what we speak and write clear, tidy, and packed with significance.

In contrast, shoddy verbal packaging results in vagueness, sloppiness, and confusion. A good understanding of grammatical phraseology, clause-ology, and sentence structure can help you keep your statements from coming apart at the seams.

This chapter deals with the word combinations known as phrases, clauses, and sentences and shows how these word groups can be properly combined with one another.

Phrases 101

You probably know already that a *phrase* is a string of words that's not quite enough to make a complete sentence. In fact, phrases are groups of words that can function as parts of speech, including nouns, verbs, adverbs, and adjectives. Unlike clauses and sentences, phrases do not contain both a subject and a verb, though they may contain either one or the other.

Parse Words

A **phrase** is a grouping of words that does not contain both a subject and a predicate, but may function as a part of speech such as a noun, verb, adjective, or adverb.

Here are some phrases used as various parts of speech:

> an eminent authority on volcanoes (noun phrase)
>
> skipping blithely through the hollyhocks (noun or adjectival phrase)
>
> green and blue with brown speckles (adjectival phrase)
>
> should have been finished (verb phrase)

with all of the bells and whistles (adverbial or adjectival phrase)

Phrases can function grammatically as individual parts of speech, even though they are made up of words that may belong to various other parts of speech. Recognizing phrases as parts of speech is useful in figuring out how sentences are put together. Divide and conquer!

Sharpening Your Clause

A *clause* is a group of words that contains both a subject and a predicate. A clause may be a complete sentence unto itself or part of a larger sentence. In fact, a single sentence may have one, two, or more clauses. Here's a clause that's also a complete sentence:

> The rain made the path muddy and the porch slippery.

Parse Words

A **clause** is a grouping of words that contains a subject and a predicate and that may be a complete sentence unto itself or combine with other clauses into a larger sentence.

You can tell this sentence is made up of only one clause because it has only one subject, "the rain," and only one predicate, "made the path muddy and the porch slippery." Don't be fooled by the presence of two objects, "path" and "porch," and two object complements, "muddy" and "slippery"; the sentence is made up of only one clause.

Here's a sentence made up of two clauses:

> Children who drink a lot of sweet soft drinks tend to eat very little fresh fruit.

You can tell this sentence has two clauses because it has two subjects and two predicates. Can you spot them? It's a little tricky. The two subjects are "children" and "who." The two predicates are "drink a lot of sweet soft drinks" and "tend to eat very little fresh fruit." The two different clauses, then, are "children tend to eat very little fresh fruit" and "who drink a lot of sweet soft drinks."

Dependency Issues

Clauses may be independent or dependent. An *independent clause* is one that makes a complete sentence on its own. A *dependent clause*, also called a subordinate clause, cannot stand on its own but is usually a modifier—adverbial or adjectival—that has its own subject and verb. Alternatively, a dependent clause may function as a noun—either the subject or the object of a sentence. An independent clause may join with another independent clause or with a dependent clause in a sentence On the other hand, a dependent clause must join with an independent clause to form a sentence.

> **Parse Words** _____
>
> An **independent clause** contains both
> a subject and a verb and requires no
> additional information to constitute a sen-
> tence, although it may be combined with
> other clauses to make a longer sentence.
> A **dependent clause** contains a subject
> and a verb but cannot form a complete
> sentence on its own.

Dependent clauses are either adverbial, adjectival,
or noun clauses. Adjective clauses modify nouns or
pronouns that are part of the independent clause.
All adjective clauses begin with one of the following
relative pronouns: *who, whom, whose, which,* or *that.*

Here's an example of a sentence that consists of
an independent clause followed by an adjectival
dependent clause:

> I've always admired Kelly, who never seems to
> get angry no matter what.

Here, the word *who* should tip you off that the
clause to follow modifies the noun *Kelly.* If a
clause is a modifier, it has to be dependent.

Here's a sentence that has a dependent adjective
clause in the middle of an independent clause:

> The claim on the cereal box that Pog-O's
> cereal jumps up and down when it touches
> milk isn't true at all.

The independent clause could stand on its own as a sentence:

> The claim on the cereal box isn't true at all.

The dependent clause requires more information:

> that Pog-O's cereal jumps up and down when it touches milk

Notice that without the word *that*, this dependent clause would be an independent clause. You might say the relative pronoun *that* makes the clause subordinate (dependent). In other words, *that* turns a clause that could otherwise stand on its own into a modifier of another clause. In fact, with just a little tweaking, the independent clause could be subordinated to the dependent clause, like this:

> Even though it isn't true, the cereal box claims that Pog-O's cereal jumps up and down when it touches milk.

The point is that it's the grammatical structure of a clause, not the information it contains, that determines whether it's dependent or independent. Any piece of information could serve either as the main point of a sentence or as a supporting or qualifying detail. It's the writer, of course, who decides how to structure clauses and sentences according to the importance of each idea and bit of information in the grand scheme of what he or she has to say.

Pack your main ideas and most important points into independent clauses, and put contextualizing details into dependent clauses.

OK! **Grammar Rules, OK!** _____

All dependent clauses begin with a marker word such as a relative pronoun (*who, whom, whose, which,* or *that*), a subordinating conjunction (*although, because, whether, while,* etc.), or a conjunctive adverb (*besides, incidentally, moreover,* etc.) that indicates the whole clause modifies some other word or group of words in the sentence.

Before, After, and In Between

An adjective clause is a dependent clause that modifies a noun or a pronoun belonging to an independent clause. Similarly, an adverbial clause is a dependent clause that modifies a verb belonging to an independent clause. An adverbial clause begins with a subordinating conjunction such as *after, although, as, because, before, even, if, once, since, though, unless, until, when,* and *while;* there are many others as well. (You can read about subordinating conjunctions in Chapter 6.)

Here are some adverbial clauses all by themselves. Notice they have their own subject and verb but require additional information before they're considered complete sentences:

after the sun goes down

whenever I see you wearing that ridiculous hat

although some dogs may appear more intelligent than others

until the crack of dawn

OK! **Grammar Rules, OK!** _____

> Adverb clauses can come before or after the independent clauses they belong with. When they appear at the beginning of a sentence, they should be followed by a comma. If they appear at the end of a sentence, no extra punctuation is necessary.

Clauses, Essentially

Do you feel comfortable with your solid grasp of the distinction between independent and dependent clauses? Awesome! Now get ready for a mind-boggling nuance: a clause may be dependent yet essential; a clause may be independent yet incomplete. I'll explain just as soon as your head stops reeling!

Essential clauses (also known as restrictive clauses or necessary clauses) are dependent clauses that supply necessary information without which the sentences they belong to wouldn't make sense. They are not syntactically (structurally) necessary, but they are semantically (meaningfully) necessary because they contain information that completes the idea presented in the independent clause.

Parse Words

An **essential clause** or phrase is one that is not structurally necessary but is a semantically necessary part of the sentence. Without it, the sentence wouldn't form an accurate statement.

Here's an example:

> People who have a heart condition should not take this medicine.

In this sentence, the main clause has everything it needs structurally to form a complete sentence. The problem is that sentence doesn't make accurate sense:

> People should not take this medicine.

The essential clause "who have a heart condition" supplies necessary information.

One way to think about the difference between an essential clause and a nonessential clause is to consider that the information in a nonessential clause could just as easily and correctly go in another sentence. An essential clause, in contrast, has to be part of the sentence it belongs to. (By the way, in addition to clauses, phrases may be essential or nonessential.)

Let's compare a sentence with an essential clause to another with a nonessential clause:

> *Essential clause:* Birds that lay eggs in other birds' nests are considered parasites.
>
> *Nonessential clause:* Birds, including the ones that congregate at backyard feeders, compete with each other for food.

Note that essential clauses are not set apart from the rest of the sentence by commas, whereas nonessential clauses are. In fact, sometimes commas are the only clue available as to whether a clause is essential or not. Take a look at these two nearly identical sentences:

> The teacher gave low grades to all the students who had difficulty with the exam.
>
> The teacher gave low grades to all the students, who had difficulty with the exam.

Can you figure out the semantic and syntactic distinction between these sentences? The first sentence ends with an essential clause, "who had difficulty with the exam." The second sentence ends with the same clause set apart by a comma, which indicates that the clause is nonessential. The first sentence indicates that the teacher gave low grades to some of the students—those who had difficulty with the exam. The second sentence indicates that the teacher gave low grades to all the students—all of whom had difficulty with the exam.

If you're with me so far on the difference between essential and nonessential modifiers, you're ready for the crowning distinction. It's not a vital issue but a somewhat subtle touch you can throw in to show what a discriminating sense of grammar you have: use *that* where appropriate for essential clauses and phrases. For nonessentials, use *which*.

Both these examples are correct:

A house on our block, which has old slate shingles, is going up for sale.

All the houses in our neighborhood that were built more than 50 years ago are going up for sale.

OK! Grammar Rules, OK!

Nonessential clauses and phrases should be set apart from the rest of the sentence by commas. Essential clauses and phrases should not. Use *which* after a comma to introduce nonessential clauses and phrases. Use *that* without a comma to introduce essential modifiers.

Clauses in Concert

In theory, there's no limit to the number of clauses that can be put together in a single sentence. In fact, during ancient times, orators prided themselves on their ability to string together clauses into long, convoluted sentences known as "periods." (That's where the name of the punctuation mark comes from.) These days, most writers and speakers form sentences made up of no more than three clauses.

Grammarians have helpfully identified different kinds of sentences based on the number and kind of clauses they are made of:

- A *simple sentence* is made of a single independent clause.
- A *compound sentence* is made of two or more independent clauses.
- A *complex sentence* is made of at least one independent clause together with at least one dependent clause.
- A *compound-complex sentence* is made of at least two independent clauses and at least one dependent clause.

Grammarians call the combining of two grammatically similar things, such as two independent clauses, *coordination*. In contrast, the combining of two non-equivalent things, such as an independent and a dependent clause, is called *subordination*. Proper coordination and subordination depend on how and whether the two things being joined belong together.

Parse Words

> **Coordination** is the relation of two grammatically similar words or word groups. **Subordination** is the relation of two dissimilar word groups.

Problems arise when two clauses are brought together that should not be. This problem results in faulty coordination. Here's an example:

The lawnmower broke down again, and I'm
watching TV this afternoon.

Here two clauses are joined that have no apparent
logical connection. The clauses should either be
separated into two sentences or the sentence should
be revised to show a stronger relationship between
the two clauses. Here's a revision that fixes the
faulty coordination:

The lawnmower broke down again, so I'm
watching TV this afternoon.

The revision establishes a logical relationship
between the two clauses that suggests why they
belong together.

OK! **Grammar Rules, OK!**

Two independent clauses can be
joined in a sentence either by a coordinating conjunction preceded by a comma or
by a semicolon.

Similarly, when the logical relationship between
joined dependent and independent clauses is
unclear, faulty subordination results, as in this
example:

Because you ate too many brownies, you
shouldn't blame the one who baked them.

The subordinating conjunction, *because*, doesn't
express a clear, logical relationship between the

clauses "you ate too many brownies" and "you shouldn't blame the one who baked them." Did the baker do a bad job and deserve blame from someone who didn't eat too many brownies? Or does eating too many brownies constitute unjust cause for blaming the baker rather than oneself? The sentence should be revised to read as either of the following:

> Even though you ate too many brownies, you shouldn't blame the one who baked them.

> Because it was you who ate too many brownies, you shouldn't blame the one who baked them.

Defrag Your Sentences

Sentences that have too much going on in them often have coordination and subordination problems. In contrast, sentences without enough ... Broken cookies. Batteries not included. A hole in the bucket. Pieces of a dream. These sentence fragments just don't deliver the whole package, and when something's missing from your sentences ...

Grammar Jammer

Not all sentence fragments are mistakes. Writers often use fragments deliberately to surprise the reader or to produce a conversational tone.

To be complete, a sentence needs to have at least one subject and one predicate—that's a noun and a verb stated as an independent clause. In other words, the noun and verb need to stand together on their own. A complete sentence also needs a period, exclamation mark, or question mark at the end. That's it!

Subjects and predicates belong together. They were made for each other. So when one or the other turns up missing, it's a sad day in Grammarville. Usually there's a common sentence fragment problem to blame.

OK! **Grammar Rules, OK!**

For a sentence to be complete, it must have a subject and a predicate.

Dependent Clause in Need of a Subject

If a clause is dependent, it can't stand on its own as a complete sentence. Take a look at this fragment:

Whenever I see purple spots before my eyes.

Of course, without the *whenever*, this sentence would be complete, with *I* as the subject and *see* as the predicate. But the *whenever* makes this phrase a dependent clause in need of a subject to modify, which, in turn, needs a predicate of its own. Here's a complete sentence:

Whenever I see purple spots before my eyes, I stick out my tongue to see if it's raining grape juice.

Here, the original sentence fragment turns out to be a dependent clause modifying the subject, which is the second *I*, which has *stick out* as a predicate.

The point is, not all nouns are subjects and not all verbs are predicates. It depends on whether they stand alone or whether they modify some other element. (Feel free to flip back to the section on dependent and independent clauses earlier in this chapter for clarification.)

Margin of Error

Imagine what would happen if someone put a stop sign in the middle of the block with no intersection in sight. Stop? Why? We haven't gotten anywhere yet! It would be confusing to say the least. It would be sort of like what happens when writers put a period between two clauses that belong in the same sentence.

Accept the Exception

Now that you have the basic idea behind sentence fragments, it's a good time to think about exceptions to the rule. Think! Think hard! Think about sentences like this one, which have no stated subjects! It's called an imperative sentence because it takes the form of a command to do something. The subject is always *you* and is often implied rather than actually stated.

You is the subject, and *think* is the predicate in the three imperative sentences in the preceding paragraph. Even though the subject is only implied, even a one-word imperative sentence is complete, as in "Think!" or "Understand!"

Now slack off and bask in the luminous glow of your scintillating intelligence! Or if you like, you can flip to the section in Chapter 4 on verb moods. The imperative mood is one of three, including indicative and subjunctive.

The Least You Need to Know

- ◆ A phrase is a grouping of words that does not contain both a subject and a predicate, but may function as a part of speech such as a noun, verb, adjective, or adverb.

- ◆ A clause is a grouping of words that contains a subject and a predicate and that may be a complete sentence unto itself or combine with other clauses into a larger sentence.

- ◆ An independent clause is one that could make up a complete sentence on its own. A dependent clause, also called a subordinate clause, cannot stand on its own, but is actually a modifier or a noun.

- ◆ To be complete, a sentence needs to have at least one subject and one predicate.

Chiming In: Agreement, Consistency, and Parallelism

In This Chapter

- ❖ Subject-verb agreement
- ❖ Consistency in person and number
- ❖ Parallel construction

Good grammar, properly abided by, results in a harmonious state of verbal affairs in which the logic of structure dovetails with the logic of meaning. When properly inflected, the parts of speech reinforce one another, yet provide such pleasing variation that the "ding dong, dong ding" of language calls us like a musical doorbell we can't help but answer, just in case Truth and Beauty have come by for a visit, bringing sandwiches.

Mmmmm, sandwiches …

But if there are subject-verb agreement problems
… if there are unnecessary pronoun shifts … if
there's faulty parallelism … then the words don't
sound so good and the meaning doesn't get across
so clearly.

Can't We Get Along?

Subject-verb agreement is crucial to good grammar. As you might remember, the subject is the
noun or pronoun that carries out the action
described by the verb. A subject in the singular
form requires a corresponding verb in the singular
form. A plural subject requires a plural verb.

That sounds pretty straightforward, doesn't it?
Sometimes it can be tricky to tell whether the
subject counts as singular or plural, though. In
fact, myriad situations can trip people up. The following sections present a whole list of these trou-
blemaking situations, together with examples of
what to do in each case.

OK! **Grammar Rules, OK!** _____
The plural form of many (but not all)
nouns ends in the letter *s*. The singular
form of many (but not all) verbs also ends
in the letter *s*. As a result, you may get an
s form for either the subject or the verb,
but never for both.

Compound Subjects

Compound subjects consist of two or more nouns
or pronouns joined by the conjunction *and*. Count
them as plural, as in this example:

> Yellow and green are my favorite colors.

Subjects with *Either ... Or*

Sometimes plural nouns and singular nouns are
joined by the correlative conjunctions *either ... or*,
neither ... nor, or *not only ... but also*. In these cases,
the verb should agree with the word closest to it:

> Either Betty or her sisters need to have a talk
> with Uncle Morris.

> Not only the peas but also the roast tastes like
> talcum powder.

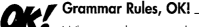 **Grammar Rules, OK!** _____

> Whenever the personal pronoun *I* is
> used as part of a compound subject, state
> it last:
>
> > He and I went to the game.
>
> Similarly, when *me* is used as part of
> a compound object, state it last also:
>
> > They had been looking for Alice,
> > Amir, and me.

Collective Nouns

Collective nouns such as *group*, *batch*, *gang*, and *committee* refer to groups of things or people, but they almost always count as singular, as in this example:

> The committee was divided on the question of whom to elect as chair.

Some sources, however, say it's acceptable to use collective nouns with plural verb forms when the people and things that form the group act as individuals, as in this example:

> The flock were scattered in all different directions.

Plural Words for Individual Things

Some things are designated by plural forms even though they are single things, such as *scissors*, *pliers*, *pants*, *coveralls*, *eyeglasses*, and *binoculars*. These words take plural verbs:

> These binoculars are getting fogged up.

Use a singular verb, however, with *pair of pants*, *pair of scissors*, etc.:

> This pair of binoculars is getting fogged up.

Plural Words for Noncount Nouns

Noncount nouns are words for things that can't be counted, such as *goo* and *happiness*. Some noncount nouns have plural forms, including *politics, physics, economics, measles, mumps, herpes,* and *news.* Despite their plural form, these words should be treated as singular:

> Physics is my most difficult subject.

 Parse Words

> Noncount **nouns** are words for things that can't be counted, such as *reality* and *dust.*

Plural Words for Proper Nouns

Proper nouns are names for people, places, and other one-of-a-kind things, including titles and the names of companies. They should be treated as singular even when they take plural forms, as in these examples:

> My friend Aces is a good card player.
>
> *Pride and Prejudice* is required reading in many English programs.

Sports teams, however, should be treated as plural, even when they have a singular noun for a name.

> The Utah Jazz are struggling this year.

Words for Amounts

Amounts should be treated as singular, as in these examples:

Ten years is a long time.

Four dollars is all I have.

Indefinite Pronouns

Indefinite pronouns include words such as *all*, *any*, *each*, *either*, *every*, *neither*, *none*, *nothing*, *one*, and *some*. Some indefinites, namely *each* and *every*, are always singular and take singular verbs:

Each of the dogs is wearing a collar.

This rule holds true for the pronouns *everyone* and *everybody*, which are always singular and take singular verbs.

Everyone should love her country.

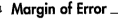

Margin of Error

You might think the phrase *more than one* should be treated as a plural subject. In fact, it's singular:

More than one battery fits into the flashlight.

Other indefinite pronouns, including *all*, *most*, *none*, and *some*, can be used with either singular or plural verbs, depending on the antecedent (the noun the pronoun refers to). Here are some examples:

Most [of the time] is taken up with driving.

Most [of the bananas] are too ripe.

None [of my hopes] were realized.

None [of the performance] was worthwhile.

Similarly, fractions and percentages can be singular or plural, depending on what they refer to:

A quarter [of the milk] was spilt.

A quarter [of the cheese puffs] were eaten.

 **Grammar Rules, OK!**

Mathematical sums should be treated as singular and given singular verbs:

Two plus two is four.

Twenty-seven divided by three is nine.

Linking Verbs

Linking verbs relate subjects to their complements by stating an equivalence or similarity. For example, in the sentence "That dog seems friendly." the linking verb *seems* relates the subject, *dog*, to its complement, *friendly*. Linking verbs include the forms of the verbs *appear, be, become, feel, grow, look, remain, seem,* and *taste.*

Linking verbs often link singular subjects with plural complements and link plural subjects with singular complements. When they do, the verb should agree with the subject rather than the complement, as in these examples:

Olives are my favorite food.

My favorite food is olives.

Here and *There* as Subjects

When the subject of the sentence is *here* or *there*, the verb may be singular or plural, depending on whether the subject complement is singular or plural:

There is a problem with the computer.

There are a number of ways to deal with it.

The Shift Is Off

Using the language well involves following rules, but also making innumerable choices. Many of these choices aren't governed by convention but are simply a matter of personal preference. After you make a choice, stick with it for the sake of clarity and consistency. Unnecessary *shifts* tend to confuse matters.

Parse Words _____

Shifts are inappropriate changes in grammatical form, usually in person or number, that take place within a sentence or over the course of several sentences.

Sorry, Wrong Number

Unnecessary grammatical shifts are common problems, especially pronoun shifts involving person and number. Here's an example of an unnecessary number shift from singular to plural:

> To succeed in baseball today, a pitcher has to contend with extremely good hitters. To do so, they need a good fastball and at least two effective off-speed pitches.

Here, the writing shifts from the singular noun, *a pitcher* to the plural pronoun, *they*. The statement should be revised so the pronoun agrees with its antecedent (either "a pitcher has to contend ... he or she needs a good fastball" or "pitchers have to contend ... they need a good fastball").

Here's another unnecessary shift in person:

> When someone comes in from the rain, they should wipe their feet.

The sentence should be revised so both pronouns are either plural or singular (either "someone comes ... he or she should wipe his or her feet" or "people come ... they should wipe their feet").

Shifty Characters

Shifts in pronoun person are a common problem as well, especially shifts between *you* and *one*. Here's an example of a shift in person:

> Whenever one does laundry, it's a good idea to sort it first; otherwise, you could end up with pink underwear.

Here the subject shifts unnecessarily from *one* to *you*. The statement should be revised for consistency (either "one does laundry ... one could end up" or "you do laundry ... you could end up").

Straight Lines

Ever see an old building with walls, floors, and ceilings that weren't square? It can make you wonder how much longer it's going to remain standing before it collapses on itself. Meanwhile, it looks pretty strange. Parallel construction is a good thing not only in buildings, but in speech and writing as well. The grammatical problem of faulty parallelism is a little bit like a crooked building. The structure isn't as straight and solid as it should be.

Parallel construction refers to the consistency of grammatical form among similar elements, such as entries in a list of words, phrases, or clauses. These elements are joined by the coordinating conjunction *and* or by the correlative conjunctions *both ... and, either ... or,* and *whether ... or.*

Parse Words

Parallel construction is the grammatical consistency of functionally or conceptually equivalent words, phrases, clauses, or sentences.

Skewed Construction

Here's an example of faulty parallelism, with some suggested revisions:

> *Incorrect:* I like swimming, sailing, and to relax with friends.

> *Correct:* I like to swim, sail, and relax with friends.

> *Correct:* I like swimming, sailing, and relaxing with friends.

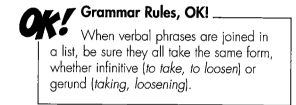

Grammar Rules, OK!

When verbal phrases are joined in a list, be sure they all take the same form, whether infinitive (*to take, to loosen*) or gerund (*taking, loosening*).

Here's more failure to align, with the aligned version following:

> *Incorrect:* Let's decide whether to eat now or if we should see a movie first.

> *Correct:* Let's decide whether to eat now or see a movie first.

List 'Em Crisply

Items in a list should all take the same grammatical form, regardless of whether the list runs down the page or across. Any bullets, numbering, capitalization, or punctuation used should be consistent throughout the list. Items in a list should also be distinct from one another. Here's a list guilty of faulty parallelism on several counts:

1) eating hamburger

2. steak.

3—Fish

4 seafood

Can you spot all the problems with this list? The punctuation following the numbers, the punctuation following the entries, the capitalization, and the grammatical form of the entries are all inconsistent. In addition, *Fish* shouldn't be a separate item, because it's included under *seafood*. Here's the same list with its problems corrected:

1) hamburger

2) steak

3) seafood

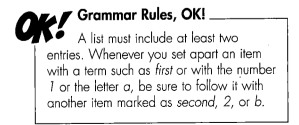

Grammar Rules, OK!

A list must include at least two entries. Whenever you set apart an item with a term such as *first* or with the number *1* or the letter *a*, be sure to follow it with another item marked as *second*, *2*, or *b*.

By the way, in general you shouldn't capitalize items in a list unless the items take the form of complete sentences. By the same token, don't use periods or other ending punctuation after items in a list unless the entries are complete sentences.

No, No Is a No-No

Agreement, consistency, and parallel form are good things, but sometimes too much is a problem, especially where negative statements are concerned. In Standard English, one negative word per clause is enough. Two negative words constitute a double negative, which is incorrect.

Grammar Jammer

In many languages, including the Romance languages, double negatives *are* correct. The negative form isn't said to negate itself when used twice in a statement; it is said to fulfill the requirements of grammatical agreement.

Here's an example of a double negative, with a revised version as well:

> *Incorrect:* I don't have nothing more to say.
>
> *Correct:* I don't have anything more to say.

The Least You Need to Know

- ◆ Nouns and verbs must agree in person and number.
- ◆ Maintain consistency in person and number, both within sentences and from sentence to sentence.
- ◆ Employ parallel construction—the grammatical consistency of functionally or conceptually equivalent words, phrases, clauses, or sentences—where appropriate.
- ◆ Avoid double negatives!

Marks of Distinction

Part 2 gets nittier and grittier by looking at the rules governing punctuation according to MLA (Modern Language Association) style. You'll find an account of the different punctuation marks used in English, including what they mean and precisely where and when to use them. In addition, you'll find discussions of common mistakes made with each mark.

Pausing for Breath

In This Chapter

- ◆ Punctuation for pause: commas, semicolons, and colons
- ◆ End marks: periods, question marks, and exclamation points

You may be surprised to learn that punctuation actually is *not* like seasoning you sprinkle into soup according to your personal tastes or your mood at the time. The purpose of punctuation is not to add flavor or let you express yourself, but to make writing easier to read and understand. It generally does so by setting off groups of words in ways that show how they are structured.

Punctuation helps compensate for the fact that written language lacks the tonal inflections—the pauses and the variations in pitch and volume—that help make speech understandable. It provides the subtle clues necessary to sort words into grammatically meaningful packages.

Among the most useful and the most misused marks of punctuation are commas, colons, and semicolons. One of the reasons they are so useful and so hard to use correctly is that they can be used under many different circumstances. This chapter maps out the terrain of the three most important within-sentence punctuation marks and also offers guidance with end-stop punctuation: periods, question marks, and exclamation points.

Comma Conundrums

Commas can be tricky. They are used to set apart certain clauses and phrases, but not others. They are used to set apart certain modifiers, but not others. The situation is somewhat complicated, but it's not hopeless! To understand when to use commas, you need to understand the grammatical structure of the words, phrases, and clauses they separate. Here's the story of when and when not to use commas.

Grammar Jammer _____

The modern comma may have evolved from a slash inserted into a line of printed text to indicate a pause by the Renaissance printer, Aldus Manutius (1449–1515).

Of the Essence

Perhaps the biggest challenge to proper comma use lies in figuring out the difference between essential and nonessential clauses and phrases. Use commas to set apart nonessential word groups, but not essential groups. You can read about this difference in detail in Chapter 7, but for now keep in mind that essential clauses and phrases contain information that, if removed, would render the sentence absurd or inaccurate. Nonessential clauses and phrases, in contrast, contain information that could be left out or moved to a separate sentence and not cause any harm to the sentence. In short, essential elements are necessary and nonessential elements aren't.

It is these nonessential modifiers—also called non-restrictive modifiers—that should be set apart with commas. Makes sense doesn't it? You can think of essential clauses and phrases as more closely related to the rest of the sentence than the nonessentials. Therefore, no comma is required to set them apart. For clauses or phrases that begin with *that* or *which*, use *that* to introduce essential clauses and phrases and *which* to introduce the nonessentials.

OK! **Grammar Rules, OK!**

Nonessential clauses and phrases should be set apart with commas. They're the ones that can be left out without changing the basic meaning of the sentence.

Take a look at the following sample sentences that contain either essential or nonessential modifiers.

Those that contain nonessential modifiers have them properly set apart by commas:

> This cat, which has only three legs, would not survive long in the wild.

> Cats that have only three legs cannot survive long in the wild.

> Everyone who wears a costume will receive a door prize.

> Joel, who didn't wear a costume, received a door prize anyway.

Comma Chameleon

Commas have many other uses in addition to setting apart nonessential modifiers. Here's a list of comma-use rules, along with some examples:

- ♦ Use commas to separate items in a series. These are called *serial commas:*

    > Let's go out dining, drinking, and dancing.

Parse Words

Serial commas are commas used to set apart items in a series of three or more.

- ♦ Do not use commas to separate items in a series when those items require internal commas. In such cases, use semicolons:

> Guest speakers include George Packam
> Pear, M.D., Ph.D.; Sylvia Bootle,
> D.D.S.; and Herman Hoot Jr.

♦ Use commas before coordinating conjunctions (*and, but, for, nor, or, so,* and *yet*) that
  join two independent clauses:

> Pandas eat almost constantly, but boa
> constrictors eat only once in several days.

Grammar Jammer

To remember all the coordinating conjunctions, you can use the mnemonic
device FANBOYS: *for, and, nor, but, or,
yet,* and *so.*

♦ Use commas to separate adjectives that
  modify the same noun equally:

> the sick, hungry dog
>
> the strange, intriguing song

♦ However, do not use commas to separate
  an adjective that modifies an adjective-noun
  grouping:

> the unemployed auto workers
>
> the leftover candied yams

♦ Use commas to set apart clauses and phrases
  that introduce a sentence or intervene
  within a sentence:

> Whatever the outcome, we'll at least
> have a good time.

Incidentally, I like your outfit.

This tomato, believe it or not, was grown in Alaska.

♦ Use commas in dates to separate the day from the year, regardless of whether the date appears as part of a sentence or separately:

April 7, 1978

February 25, 2003

They were married on July 2, 1940, in a small, white church.

Grammar Jammer

Can you imagine a book written entirely without punctuation? It's been done. New Englander Timothy Dexter (1747–1806) wrote his book, *A Pickle for the Knowing Ones*, without even a single comma or period. As if to make amends, he provided punctuation for the second edition of his book simply by adding a page filled with marks for his readers to use however they liked!

♦ Do not use a comma if the month is written between the day and the year:

7 April 1978

25 February 2003

♦ Do not use a comma to separate either months or seasons from the year:

July 1959

spring 2002

♦ Use a comma between city and state as well
as after the state when used in a sentence:

Hackensack, New Jersey

Our parents grew up in Louisville,
Kentucky, during the Great Depression.

Un-Comma'd Excellence

The conventions governing when *not* to use commas can be as helpful to know as those governing
when *to* use them. Here's a list of rules, with accom-
panying examples, for when to leave commas out:

> **Margin of Error**
>
> One of the most common mistakes
> involving commas is the comma splice, the
> incorrect use of a comma to join two sen-
> tences into one. Here's an example of this
> problem:
>
> > *Incorrect:* The accountants are taking
> > a break again, don't they have any-
> > thing better to do?
>
> Here the comma should be replaced by a
> period or a semicolon.
>
> > *Correct:* The accountants are taking a
> > break again. Don't they have anything
> > better to do?

♦ Don't use a comma between the subject and verb. Here's a sentence with a misplaced comma between the compound subject and the verb *went:*

> *Incorrect:* Donna, Ed, Miriam, and I, went to the museum.

♦ Don't use a comma between the verb and the object of the sentence. Here's a sentence with a wrongly placed comma between the verb, "hoped and prayed," and the object, "for their cause":

> *Incorrect:* They diligently hoped and prayed, for their cause.

♦ Don't use a comma to separate two parts of a compound subject, compound verb, or compound object. Here's a sentence that wrongly inserts a comma within a compound subject:

> *Incorrect:* The roving band of store clerks, and their manager were on the prowl for customers they could help.

Here's a sentence with a comma wrongly inserted within a compound verb:

> *Incorrect:* The gardeners hoed, and weeded the garden.

Here's a sentence with a comma wrongly inserted within a compound object:

> *Incorrect:* We looked all over the store for something that would relieve my headache, or help me sleep.

♦ Don't use a comma between two parallel subordinate clauses and phrases:

> *Incorrect:* Our car broke down leaving us stranded by the side of the road, waiting for a tow truck.

Here a comma is wrongly inserted between the parallel phrases, "stranded by the side of the road" and "waiting for a tow truck."

Semi-Tough

Semicolons are punctuation marks that can lend a touch of sophistication to your writing if you use them properly. You may already be aware that semicolons more strongly separate groups of words than do commas but not as strongly as periods. Semicolons are required on two common occasions. Here are the rules governing their use:

♦ As mentioned previously in this chapter, use semicolons to separate items in a list that contain commas. Semicolons make the list clearer and easier to read than it would be if commas were used both within the items and between the items:

> The three brothers were born on September 12, 1953; April 18, 1956; and March 27, 1959.

♦ Use semicolons between two independent clauses that aren't joined by a coordinating conjunction. (You can read about independent clauses in Chapter 7.)

> We appreciate your enthusiasm; however, we're not certain you have enough relevant experience.

Use a semicolon only between parallel word groups. Don't use a semicolon to join a clause with a phrase or to join a dependent clause to an independent clause. The following sentences, for example, contain unnecessary semicolons:

> I was confused by the lecture; especially the part about statistical variation.

Here the semicolon wrongly joins a clause with a phrase. It should be replaced by a comma: "… the lecture, especially …"

> We'll keep practicing; at least until we understand what we're doing wrong.

Here the semicolon wrongly joins a dependent and an independent clause. It should be replaced by a comma: "… practicing, at least until …"

Grammar Jammer

Think of commas, semicolons, and periods as three different marks of separation. Commas are used to separate nonessential phrases and clauses from the rest of the sentence; semicolons are used to separate independent clauses from one another; and periods are used to separate complete sentences from one another.

Scoping Out the Colon

The colon is that special mark that tells readers, "Here comes what you know is coming." In fact, it's rare among punctuation marks in that it can be used interchangeably with certain words. For example, *such as, including, they are,* and *that is to say* are all terms that perform a task similar to that performed by the colon.

Use a colon to announce, elaborate, or specify information that has just been introduced:

> There are three imaginary creatures in the story: a ghost, a dragon, and a genie.

> The policeman offered some good advice: "Don't hassle the police."

Don't use a colon if words in the sentence accomplish the job without it. These sentences, for example, include unnecessary colons:

> The three imaginary creatures in the story are: a ghost, a dragon, and a genie.

> The ingredients include: gin, vermouth, and a stuffed olive.

Both of these sentences should be revised by simply omitting the colon. Note that colons should never be placed after linking verbs.

> **OK!** **Grammar Rules, OK!** _____
>
> When using a semicolon or a colon
> with quotation marks, put it outside the
> marks, as in this example:
>
> He said "yes"; however, he meant "no."
>
> Note that placement of colons and semi-
> colons differs from the placement of periods
> and commas, which go inside quotation
> marks.

In addition to their chief function of introducing
explanations, details, and examples, colons have a
number of highly specialized functions. Here's a
list, with examples:

- ◆ Use a colon after the salutation in a formal
  letter:

    Dear Ms. Jaspers:

    To whom it may concern:

- ◆ Use a colon to show odds and ratios:

    odds of 3:1

    a 4:1 ratio

- ◆ Use a colon to separate hours from minutes
  when telling the time:

    12:45

    7:15

- ◆ Use a colon to separate chapter and verse in
  scriptural references:

    Job 11:8

♦ Use a colon to separate the title from the subtitle in papers and articles:

> Responding to Noise Pollution: Protesters Make Themselves Heard Above the Din

Grammar Jammer

Punctuation marks should not be confused with two other kinds of markings: typographical symbols and diacritical marks, including the *ampersand* (&), the *commercial at* (@), and the *asterisk* (*) traditionally used by typesetters. (They're also used by cartoonists to represent cursing and profanity, as when Sergeant Snorkel finds Beetle Bailey goofing off on the job and says "*%$#@&!") Diacritical marks, including the *umlaut* ("), the *tilde* (~), and the *cedilla* (ç) are marks added to letters to indicate phonetic distinctions (differences in the ways they are pronounced).

Last Stop

The ends of complete sentences are marked by three well-known marks of punctuation: the period, the question mark, and the exclamation point. Use periods at the end of declarative sentences. Use question marks at the end of questions. Use exclamation points for emphasis and to show excitement or surprise.

> ! **Grammar Jammer** _____
>
> Historians believe that the question mark evolved from letters originally used as shorthand for the Latin word *quaestio*, meaning "what." This shorthand sign was a capital Q written above a lowercase *o*. Similarly, the exclamation point evidently evolved from shorthand for the Latin word *io*, meaning "joy," which was written as a capital *I* over a lowercase *o*.

Here are some guidelines to keep in mind:

♦ Question marks can appear at the ends of fragments that ask questions as well as at the ends of complete sentences.

> Really?
>
> Toto, too?

♦ Question marks are also used within sentences, enclosed within parentheses to indicate uncertainty:

> Workshops are scheduled on Friday at 9:00, 1:00 (?), and 4:00.

♦ Don't use question marks in sentences that ask indirect questions. Use periods instead:

> A tourist asked me if I knew where to get Venezuelan stamps.

- Use exclamation points at the ends of complete sentences to show emphasis or excitement:

  > The British are coming!

- Use exclamation points at the end of exclamatory sentences and fragments. These are statements that typically begin with *how* or *what*. Often the verb and sometimes the subject of an exclamatory statement are implied rather than stated.

  > How beautiful [the sunset is]!

  > How rude [you are]!

  > What a fine mess you've gotten us into this time!

- Avoid excessive use of exclamation points, especially in formal writing!!!!!!!!!!!!!!!

Grammar Jammer

In the 1960s, New York publishing companies introduced a new punctuation mark called the *interrobang* (‽). It looks like an exclamation point superimposed onto a question mark and is intended to indicate surprise and uncertainty. It never really caught on, although some typewriter keyboards once featured it.

The Least You Need to Know

- ◆ Use commas to set off nonessential clauses and phrases, or between two independent clauses joined by a coordinating conjunction. Place the comma just before the conjunction.

- ◆ Don't use a comma between subject and verb, between verb and object, between compounded elements, or between parallel subordinate clauses or phrases.

- ◆ Use semicolons between two independent clauses not joined by a conjunction or between items in a series that contain internal commas.

- ◆ Use a colon to announce, elaborate, or specify information that has just been introduced, as well as for various more specialized uses.

- ◆ Use periods, question marks, and exclamation points to mark the ends of sentences.

Tapping the Source: Quoting and Quotations

In This Chapter

- ◆ Quotation marks
- ◆ Italics and brackets
- ◆ Ellipses and slashes

Good news! There's a great, big, wonderful world of written material out there, and you can use it in your writing. All you have to do is follow the rules that help show whose words are whose.

Dealing with your own writing can be a challenge, even when you're not incorporating other people's words into your own. Working with quotations adds to the complexity of the job, but it's well worth learning how to do. You'll be able to resurrect interesting nuggets from the past as well as join in with all the topical discussions of the present.

This chapter covers quotation marks as well as some less frequently used marks, namely italics, brackets, ellipses, and slashes. All these other marks are important, too, but quotation marks are especially worth knowing about.

You Can Quote Me

Quotation marks, as you may already be aware, are used to set apart statements made by someone else. A number of rules govern their use. Most of these are necessary, because proper quotation and citation are crucial for clarity and accuracy. In some cases, failure to identify quotations as such can result in plagiarism, the theft of another person's words.

 Margin of Error

> Strictly speaking, *quote* is a verb and should not be used as a noun to mean either *quotation* or *quotation mark*. Most people, however, find it convenient to refer both to quotations and to quotation marks as *quotes*.

Rules for quotation and citation are intended to avoid confusion over who said what as well as keep you out of legal trouble through the clear and correct attribution of statements to the people who made them. Check with an appropriate style guide for help with proper citation (see the introduction for a word about style guides). Keep reading this book for rules on the use of quotation marks.

He Said, She Said

Proper quoting is an art governed by an array of conventions. Here's what you need to know:

- ◆ Use quotation marks in pairs to enclose quoted words. Never use a single quotation mark by itself.

- ◆ Use quotation marks for direct quotations. Direct quotations are the word-for-word statements of other speakers or writers. Here is an example of a direct quotation:

    > Milton said, "Kings most commonly, though strong in legions, are but weak in arguments."

    Note that a comma should fall after "said" and before the quotation. Also note that the period belongs inside the quotation marks. In addition, note that the quoted sentence begins with a capital letter, even though the quotation is only part of the larger sentence that begins with another capital letter.

- ◆ Conclude a quotation with a comma set inside the quotation marks when the sentence continues after the quotation:

    > "Kings most commonly, though strong in legions, are but weak in arguments," unless they have skilled policymakers and diplomats.

    Or use a semicolon where appropriate, set outside the quotation mark:

    > "Kings most commonly, though strong in legions, are but weak in arguments"; and weak in patience, too.

OK! **Grammar Rules, OK!** _____

When quoting words that include a mistake (in logic, spelling, usage, punctuation, or grammar), it's often appropriate to quote the mistake as it originally appears in your source. Alert your reader to the presence of the mistake (and that you didn't make it!) by inserting the Latin word *sic*, meaning "thus," italicized and in brackets immediately after the mistake:

> He said "There's a lot of disgruntment [*sic*] among the employees."

♦ Do not quote a sentence fragment without making it a part of your own complete sentence, as in this example:

> *Correct:* Milton said that kings are "weak in arguments."

Contrast this example of an improperly quoted phrase:

> Incorrect: Milton said, "though strong in legions, are but weak in arguments."

♦ Use square brackets to set apart any words you insert within a quote:

> Milton said, "Kings most commonly [especially Charles I and Emperor Hadrian], though strong in legions, are but weak in arguments."

♦ Use square brackets also to indicate that italics have been added:

> Milton said, "Kings most commonly,
> though strong in legions, are but *weak*
> in arguments [italics added]."

OK! **Grammar Rules, OK!** _____

Whenever possible, write about
what texts say and do in the present tense,
regardless of when they were written:

the Koran says ...

People magazine makes me feel ...

In contrast, write about what people say
and do in the present only if that's when
they do it.

♦ Use an ellipsis (...) to indicate where any
  words have been left out of a quotation.

> Milton said, "Kings ... are but *weak* in
> arguments."

If you are quoting a statement that already
includes an ellipsis, and you add another
one, put yours in brackets ([...]) to indicate
it is your addition.

♦ Use single quotation marks (' ') to enclose
  quotations within quotations, as in this
  example:

> Today's paper says, "The mayor was
> heard to say, 'We need higher taxes!'"

♦ Don't use quotation marks for long quotations that go on for three or more lines

of type. Instead, start the quotation on a new line and indent the entire quotation. After quoting, resume your discussion on a new line with no indentation. Long quotations presented in this way are called *block quotations*.

Parse Words _____

A **block quotation** is a long quotation of three lines or more that is written on separate lines from the main body of text and indented from the left margin. Quotation marks are not used with block quotations.

♦ Don't use quotation marks for indirect quotations. Indirect quotations rephrase or summarize words from another source, as in this example:

> My neighbor said leaves from our yard have been blowing into his.

♦ When quotation marks conclude a sentence or nonessential element, always put the comma or period inside the quotation marks. Put any colons or semicolons outside the quotation marks. Put question marks inside quotation marks to show that a question is quoted. Put question marks outside quotation marks to show that a question is asked about a quotation. Contrast these examples:

> "Shall I compare thee to a summer's day?"
>
> Was Shakespeare thinking of Sir Philip Sidney when he has Ophelia describe Hamlet as "the glass of fashion"?

So-Call It: More Quotation Mark Uses

Quotation marks have a number of other uses apart from setting off quotations:

- Use quotation marks to identify titles of short or minor works. These include songs, short stories, magazine articles, and poems. Also use them for the titles of parts of larger works such as chapters of a book.

Margin of Error

Use quotation marks for titles of short or minor works; italicize titles of long or major works. If you're not certain whether a work is long or short, see if you can find an authoritative source that has written about it and follow the example. In any case, use one or the other, but not both.

- Use quotation marks to identify words used as jargon or slang words used for the first time:

> Whenever Grandpa used to take off his belt, we knew we were about to get another "talking to."

Marked Improvements

Several marks of punctuation are used fairly infrequently. Most people screw more brackets into their walls than they include in their writing. And no, italics are not things that come from Italy. Slashes don't necessarily draw blood, and ellipses don't have to be elliptical. Here are the basics on some of the less familiar marks of punctuation.

Bracket Club

When I talk about brackets, I mean square brackets ([ ]) as opposed to several other kinds. Parentheses are sometimes (though rarely) called "round brackets." Braces ({ }) are curly brackets, and the things that look like arrows without the stick (< >) are called angle brackets. Braces and angle brackets aren't covered in this book, as their uses are chiefly technical and mathematical.

Brackets have certain specialized uses:

- ◆ Use brackets within quotations to set apart words that have been added, as in the examples shown in the "He Said, She Said" section earlier in this chapter on quotation marks.
- ◆ Use brackets to set apart parenthetical material included within a parenthesis:

Practically all the books were damaged (but not Smith's miscellany [1823]).

A Fresh Slant on Things

Italics is a style of type that slants *like this*.

> ◆ Use italics to indicate the titles of major works, such as books, plays, operas, television shows, newspapers, and magazines.

OK! **Grammar Rules, OK!** _____

Some of you young whippersnappers may not remember, but back in the days before word processors, we used underline instead of italics. Some folks still do, even on computers. Yup. Underlining works just fine for anything you'd use italics for.

> ◆ Use italics (sparingly) to emphasize words or phrases, especially important words that might otherwise be missed.
>
>> I asked for *no* mayonnaise on my sandwich.
>
> ◆ Use italics to identify words used as words, words used in peculiar ways, or words used ironically:
>
>> I've always considered the word *diphtheria* too beautiful for such a horrible illness.
>
> ◆ Italicize words and phrases (but not whole sentences) in foreign languages.
>
>> I admire Raul's devotion to his *pueblo*.

> Be aware, however, that many foreign
> words have been adopted into English
> and so should not be italicized. Check
> a dictionary if you're unsure.

Grammar Jammer

Italic type was once called *Aldine type*
after the Renaissance printer Aldus Minu-
tius, who introduced it in 1501 with his
edition of the works of the poet Virgil,
which Aldus dedicated to Italy.

To Be Continued ...

An ellipsis indicates that a word or words have
been omitted from a quotation or that a sentence
or train of thought is unfinished or spoken with
hesitation.

Make an ellipsis by typing three periods with a
space before and after each of them (...). When
omitting an entire sentence or more, insert a
period before the ellipsis, as in this example:

> We were all tired of working so hard. ... But
> rebuilding the settlement was our only hope.

Don't use an ellipsis at the beginning of a quotation. Use one at the end of a quotation only if you
are quoting an incomplete sentence that you don't
complete outside the quotation.

Slash-ing Through

The slash (/), also called a "virgule" or a "solidus," is a somewhat specialized mark. It can be used to divide paired opposites that are presented as a single concept, such as *either/or*, *his/her*, and *East/West*. However, if the paired term is used as a modifier preceding a noun, use a hyphen instead of a slash, as in "an either-or situation."

Slashes are also used to show ratios in place of the Latin word *per*, which means "by." As you probably know, "miles/hour" means "miles per hour."

Slashes are also used to indicate line breaks in poetry when the lines are written all the way across the page. For example, here are two lines of classic English verse:

> Hickory dickory dock, / The mouse ran up the clock.

Note that a space is added before and after the slash.

The Least You Need to Know

- ◇ Use quotation marks to enclose direct quotes.
- ◇ Indicate any changes you make in material you quote through the proper use of ellipses and square brackets.
- ◇ Use brackets within quotations to enclose added material. Use brackets within parentheses to enclose an internal parenthetical phrase.

- Use italics for titles of long or major works and, occasionally, for emphasis.
- Use ellipses to show where words have been omitted.
- Use a slash to join paired opposites into a single entity.

Chapter 11

More Marks of Distinction

In This Chapter

- ◆ Hyphens
- ◆ Dashes and parentheses
- ◆ Apostrophes

When you think about it, there are quite a few different marks of punctuation, including some that have many different uses and others that are rarely used for anything. Multiple uses can pose a challenge in learning to punctuate correctly; so can highly specialized marks. But I think you're ready.

So here, at last, is where we separate the hyphens from the slashes, sort out the parentheses and apostrophes, and take meticulous account of the special little details that make good speaking and writing a precise proposition.

All Hyphened Up

Hyphens indicate when a line break occurs in the middle of a word. This was especially important to know back when most people used typewriters. They might come to the end of a line of type in the middle of a word like *incontrovertible* and need to interrupt the word to start a new line. In such cases, the hyphen should be placed between two syllables. For example, *incontro-vertible.*

When dividing words with hyphens, do so as closely to the middle as possible. Avoid leaving only one or two letters by themselves. Also try to avoid dividing the last word on the page or the last word in a paragraph. In fact, it's perfectly acceptable not to divide words at all, but rather to include shorter lines as needed.

Compounded Problems

In addition to their function of dividing words at line breaks, hyphens are used in various instances involving *compound words.* In fact, hyphens are among the subtlest and most slippery marks of punctuation when used with compound words. Authorities disagree over precisely which words should be hyphenated, so it's a good idea to consult a dictionary if you're uncertain about specific words.

Some compound words are written as a single word with no hyphen, as in *backstop, stockbroker,* and *mouthpiece;* others are usually written as two words without a hyphen, such as *back talk, stock market,* and *mouth organ;* and still others are written with a hyphen between them, as in *back-formation* and *large-scale.*

Authorities refer to these three forms of compound words as *closed, open,* and *hyphenated,* respectively. In some cases, the form depends not only on the word or words, but on how they are used. For example, the noun *ice skate* is written as two words, while the verb *to ice-skate* is hyphenated. Hyphens can be tricky. Here, however, is some general guidance.

> **Parse Words**
>
> **Compound words** are two or more words that appear together and function as a single word, usually nouns, adjectives, or adverbs.
>
> **Closed compound words** are two words joined with no space between them. **Open compound words are** two words joined with a space. As for **hyphenated compound words**—yes, they are indeed hyphenated.

Joined at the Hyphen

Use hyphens to join two nouns when both describe a single person or thing, but neither modifies the other:

> poet-scholar
>
> refrigerator-freezer

Contrast these examples where hyphens should not be used:

> death wish
>
> clam digger

In general, don't use hyphens to set apart prefixes or suffixes, as in *antifreeze, noncommittal, pre-arranged,* and *unconvinced.* However, there are exceptions to this rule (aren't there always?):

- Use a hyphen after a prefix that precedes a proper noun, as in *pre-Elizabethan.*

- Use a hyphen to separate most double vowel formations, as in *anti-inflammatory* and *re-educate.* Don't use a hyphen for *coordinate* or *cooperate.* Again, check a dictionary if you're not sure.

- Use a hyphen to distinguish a word from a similar unhyphenated word. For example, hyphenate *re-count,* meaning "count again" to distinguish it from *recount,* meaning "tell." Hyphenate *re-serve* meaning "serve again" to distinguish it from *reserve,* meaning "hold back."

- Use hyphens to join compound modifiers that might otherwise be mistaken for other parts of speech:

    over-the-counter medicines

    up-to-the-minute reporting

- Note that these and other such word groups are hyphenated when used as modifiers but are not otherwise hyphenated, as in these examples:

    I bought the medicine over the counter.

    The program claimed to report the news up to the minute.

Margin of Error

Proper hyphenation is a notoriously slippery issue! Here's what the first editors of the *Concise Oxford Dictionary* (1911) said about it in their preface:

> We have also to admit that after trying hard at an early stage to arrive at some principle that should teach us when to separate, when to hyphen, and when to unite the parts of compound words, we had to abandon the attempt as hopeless, and welter in the prevailing chaos.

♦ Use hyphens to join compound adjectives made from nouns and participles (verb forms ending in *ing* or *ed*):

    corn-fed beef

    insect-eating bird

    time-honored practice

♦ Use hyphens with compound modifiers made from numbers:

    seventeenth-century song

    third-grade student

    10-year cycle

Hang Me

Write hyphens with no space between them and the words next to them, except in the case of *suspended compounds*, where *hanging hyphens* are used. A suspended compound is a compound that is interrupted in the middle, usually by a parallel compound element.

Parse Words _____

A **suspended compound** is a pair of compounded words that have an intervening word or words in the middle. They should be joined with a **hanging hyphen,** which is a hyphen that has a space after it.

Here are some examples of suspended compounds with hanging hyphens in them:

> nine- and ten-year-olds
>
> eighteenth- and nineteenth-century fashion
>
> first- and secondhand accounts

Clean Breaks

Speakers and writers continually face dilemmas concerning when, where, and whether to offer information. Supplemental information can be extremely helpful, even though it may not be necessary to the train of thought. That's why it's nice when readers can tell when the flow gets interrupted. Certain marks of punctuation, namely parentheses and dashes, help clarify the difference between the main ideas and things added by the way.

Inside Information

Supplemental information inserted into a sentence is commonly set apart with parentheses. Parentheses may be used to set apart single words, phrases, clauses, or even one or more complete sentences. The word *parentheses* (plural) or *parenthesis* (singular) comes from a Greek word meaning "to put in beside." The word *parenthesis* may also refer to a parenthetical statement, regardless of whether parentheses are used to set it apart.

Parse Words

A **parenthesis** (plural: *parentheses*) is one of a pair of punctuation marks or a statement inserted into a train of thought that is typically placed between them.

When using parentheses, you should punctuate both the parenthetical insertion and the rest of the sentence as you ordinarily would. If the parentheses conclude a sentence, place a period afterward. If parentheses include a sentence, place a period inside them.

> There were too many to count (probably more than a thousand).

> Doris had plans to change careers. (Her mother secretly hoped she would stay at her old job.)

(Em) Dash It

Not all dashes are created equal. Some are long; others are short. The long ones are called "em dashes" because they are the width of the capital letter *M*. The short ones are called "en dashes" because they are only as wide as the capital letter *N*. En dashes have different uses from em dashes.

> ### Grammar Jammer
>
> When people talk about dashes without specifying which kind they mean, they're probably referring to em dashes.

Em dashes (-- or —) can be used in much the same way as parentheses to set apart inserted explanations or interruptions. Use em dashes to convey emphasis or emotion; use parentheses to convey a neutral attitude. Contrast these two examples:

> In the summer of 1973—I'll never forget it!— few people had air conditioners.

> We filled three orders today (one was quite large) before taking the rest of the afternoon off.

Parentheses must always be used in pairs. Dashes may be used in pairs or singly to mark interruptions within sentences. They are formed on a typewriter or most word processors by hitting the hyphen key twice with no space between.

Margin of Error

Dashes mark unusually decisive breaks within sentences, so they should be used sparingly. Use no more than two in a sentence.

Dashes are used to attach sentence fragments to complete sentences, as in this example:

> Hunger, sickness, fatigue—Binky suffered every kind of hardship.

Dashes can also be used in place of commas to separate intervening clauses and phrases. Commas, however, should be your first option. Use dashes for extra clarity to set apart word groups that already contain commas, as in this example:

> The whole group—teacher, tour guide, and students—waited in the wrong line for an hour.

(En) Dash It

En dashes are used chiefly to show when two numbers indicate a range including everything that comes between them. For example, 2–7 means "two through seven"; 8:15–9:45 means "from 8:15 until 9:45."

En dashes are also used on the rare occasions when it's necessary to combine open and hyphenated compound words into bigger compounds. Here are some examples:

a Jack Johnson–Jim Jackson collaboration

a shaggy-dog–storyteller

Which reminds me of an interesting story ... Oh, never mind! Let's go on to the next section.

Turned Up Missing

Then there's the apostrophe, which is used chiefly to show possession and to form contractions.

Contractual Obligations

In contractions, the apostrophe shows where a letter is omitted, as in these examples:

cannot = can't

will not = won't

it is = it's

'em = them

yes'm = yes ma'am = yes madam

Avoid the use of contractions in formal writing. Instead, spell out the words.

> **Grammar Jammer**
>
> The possessive form made with 's (apostrophe s) originated as a contraction of the word *his*. For example, "Jacob's book" can be thought of as a contraction of the old-fashioned phrase, "Jacob, his book."

Having It All

Various rules govern the use of the apostrophe to show possession. Here's a list of them:

- ◆ Show possession by adding 's to the end of the singular noun that does the possessing:

    the dog's collar

    a day's work

    Boris's cooking

- ◆ Add only an apostrophe (not another *s*) to show possession of a plural noun ending in *s*:

    the flies' buzzing

    the leaves' colors

    the students' test

    the Smolenskis' yard

- ◆ For plural nouns that don't end in s, add 's:

    the oxen's yoke

    the women's team

    the media's hype

- ◆ To show that several nouns possess a thing or things in common, punctuate only the final noun in the series:

    Edna, Boris, and Bill's presentation

    the mouse, the cat, and the dog's cartoon

- ◆ To show that several nouns possess the same things individually, punctuate each one:

    Gloria's and Shana's clothes

    rich people's and poor people's problems

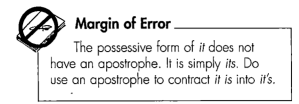

Margin of Error _____

The possessive form of *it* does not have an apostrophe. It is simply *its*. Do use an apostrophe to contract *it is* into *it's*.

◆ No apostrophes are necessary to make numbers, abbreviations, and certain words plural:

the 1950s

the M.D.s

no ifs, ands, or buts

The Least You Need to Know

◆ Use hyphens to join some compounds, but not others.

◆ Parentheses and dashes are both used to separate information inserted into the main train of thought. Parentheses are neutral; dashes suggest emotion or emphasis.

◆ Apostrophes indicate missing letters in contractions and also show possession.

Grammar Glossary

Grammarians use quite a few specialty words to refer to words, word groupings, and the various relationships they form. Here's a list of them, together with definitions.

absolute phrase   A modifier made from a verbal phrase that modifies everything else in the sentence:

> Spot having eaten, I fixed my own dinner.

Here "Spot having eaten" is an absolute phrase.

active voice   A form of predication in which the subject caries out the action described by the verb, as in "Kids ate the cake." *Contrast* passive voice.

adjective   A part of speech used to modify nouns and pronouns.

adverb   A part of speech used to modify verbs, adjectives, and other adverbs. Adverbs typically end in *ly*.

agreement   The correspondence of different parts of speech in terms of person and number. Subjects and verbs must agree (squirrels eat, a squirrel eats), as must nouns and pronouns (Caroline ate her breakfast; George inhaled his).

antecedent   The noun to which a pronoun refers. In the sentence, "The dog chased its tail." the noun, *dog*, is the antecedent of the pronoun, *it*.

appositive phrase An adjectival phrase not structurally necessary to the sentence that explains or
identifies the noun it follows:

> Mount Everest, the highest mountain, is called
> Chomolungma in Tibetan.

Here "the highest mountain" is an appositive phrase.

article A part of speech that determines nouns by
coming before it to show whether it is definite (*the*
pistachio, *the* ton of bricks) or indefinite (*a* bookshelf, *an* opportunity).

auxiliary verb *See* helping verb.

block quotation A quotation of three lines or
more that is written on lines separate from the main
body of text and indented from the left margin.
Quotation marks are not used with block quotations.

case The form taken by nouns and pronouns
depending on whether they are objective (me), sub-
jective (I), or possessive (my, mine).

clause A grouping of words that contains a subject
and a predicate and that may be a complete sentence
unto itself or may combine with other clauses into a
larger sentence. *Compare* phrase.

collective noun A noun that refers to a group of
things or people, such as *batch, family, flock, committee,* and *pile.*

common noun A noun that refers to things that
are considered the same as others of their kind, such
as *tree. Compare* proper noun.

comparative form The adjectival and adverbial
form used to compare two things formed by adding
er to the end of the base form of most adjectives
(such as *tall, taller*) and by changing the *ly* ending of
adverbs to *lier* (such as *lovely, lovelier*). The comparative form can also be made by using the words *more*

or *less* with the adverb or adjective. *Compare* positive form.

complement   A noun or adjective in a sentence containing a linking verb that is neither the subject nor the object of the sentence. A subject complement modifies the subject:

The weather was cold.

Here *cold* is the complement of the subject *weather*.

An object complement modifies the object:

We sanded the floor smooth.

Here *smooth* is the complement of the object *floor*.

complex sentence   A sentence that includes at least one dependent and at least one independent clause.

compound form   A group of words that function together as a single part of speech:

A dog, a cat, and a rat walked into a bar.

Here "A dog, a cat, and a rat" is the compound subject of the sentence.

compound-complex sentence   A sentence that includes at least two independent clauses and at least one dependent clause.

conjugation   The practice of inflecting verbs through all the forms of person and tense.

conjunction   A part of speech that relates one part of a sentence to one another and joins words and phrases. Coordinating conjunctions include *and, but, or, nor,* and *yet;* subordinating conjunctions include *if, because, although,* and *until.*

conjunctive adverb   An adverb that joins two independent clauses in a logical relationship. They include *also, anyway, besides, consequently, finally, however, nevertheless,* and *similarly.*

coordinating conjunctions Words such as *and*, *but*, *or*, and *yet* that join and relate parts that are grammatically similar.

coordination The grammatical relation of two grammatically similar words or word groups.

correlative conjunction Paired conjunctions that join and relate equivalent words or word groups. They include *as ... as, either ... or, not ... but*, and *whether ... or*.

count noun A word that may take a plural or a singular form for a distinct individual thing that may be counted. *Fleas, mountain*, and *widget* are examples. *Contrast* noncount noun.

declarative mood *See* indicative mood.

definite article A noun determiner that points to a noun that either has been introduced already or the specificity of which is understood. The word *the* is the only definite article in English.

demonstrative pronoun A pronoun that refers to things far away or close by, including *this* and *that*.

dependent clause A clause (containing a subject and a verb) that cannot form a complete sentence on its own but modifies an independent clause:

I don't want to go unless they have chutney.

Here "unless they have chutney" is a dependent clause modifying the independent clause "I don't want to go."

direct object A noun or pronoun that receives the action described by the verb:

We ate shrimp.

Here *shrimp* is a direct object. *Contrast* indirect object.

essential clause or phrase A modifying word group that is not structurally necessary but is a semantically necessary part of the sentence. Without it, the sentence wouldn't form an accurate statement:

Anyone who arrives late will be left behind.

Here "who arrives late" is an essential clause modifying the subject "anyone."

gerund A verb form that functions as a noun in which *ing* is added to the base verb, as in *running, elaborating,* etc.

hanging hyphen A hyphen that has a space after it because it joins two words that are interrupted by another word or words: *mid- to upper 50s.*

helping verb A verb combined with the main verb to create the complete verb: *may have expired; will proceed.* Here *may have* and *will* are helping verbs.

idiom A conventionally accepted word or phrase that does not obey grammatical rules and cannot be literally translated into other languages, such as "Hold up your end of the bargain."

imperative mood A command form of verbs used when telling someone to do something. The base form of the verb is used, and the subject is usually implied rather than stated. "Go slowly." and "Please respond by telephone." are sentences with verbs in the imperative mood. *Compare* indicative mood and subjunctive mood.

indefinite articles The noun determiners *a* and *an,* used to introduce nonspecific nouns.

indefinite pronoun A pronoun that refers to nonspecific things, including *all, any, each, anyone, anybody, someone, somebody, everyone, everybody, everything, nothing, one,* and *either.*

independent clause A clause (containing both a subject and a verb) that requires no additional information to constitute a sentence. It may be combined with other clauses to make a longer sentence:

I don't want to go unless they have chutney.

Here "I don't want to go" is an independent clause.

indicative mood   The most common verb mood used when saying how things are. Such sentences as "Cows eat grass." and "The bank tellers wore ridiculous costumes." have verbs in the indicative mood. *Compare to* imperative mood and subjunctive mood.

indirect object   A noun placed after a transitive verb and before a direct object that answers the question "To whom?" "For whom?" or "To what?":

We fed breadcrumbs to the ducks.

Here *ducks* is the indirect object. *Contrast* direct object.

infinitive   The verb form in which the base verb is preceded by the preposition *to*, as in, "to inquire," "to be," and "to climb."

inflection   The changing of parts of speech into various forms.

interjection   A word, phrase, or sound inserted as an exclamation.

interrogative pronoun   A pronoun that asks a question, including *how, whom, where, when,* and *which.*

intransitive verb   A verb that does not take an object and does not direct the action it describes beyond the subject:

Cats sleep most of the day.

Here *sleep* is an intransitive verb. *Compare to* transitive verb.

linking verb   A verb such as *be, become, look, sound,* and *seem* that relates the subject of a sentence to the subject complement, suggesting similarity or equivalence between the two.

main clause   *See* independent clause.

mass noun   *See* noncount noun.

modal verb   A helping verb that expresses a degree of inclination or ability. *Can, could, may, might, shall,* and *should* are modal verbs.

modifier   An adjective, adverb, or adjectival or adverbial phrase used to describe or qualify other words and phrases.

mood of the verb   *See* verb mood.

necessary clause or phrase   *See* essential clause or phrase.

noncount noun   A word for a thing that can't be counted, such as *reality* and *dust.*

nonessential clause or phrase   A word group that can be omitted from a sentence without undermining its meaning:

> Black-and-white TV sets, once common, are now hard to find.

Here *once common* is a nonessential phrase.

noun   A part of speech that stands for a person, place, or thing.

noun determiner   A word that indicates that a noun must follow. Articles and some pronouns and adjectives can be noun determiners, as can cardinal numbers.

object   A noun or pronoun that receives rather than directs the action of the verb:

> Grandma likes to swat flies.

Here *flies* is the object. *Compare* subject.

object case   The form of nouns and pronouns that receives the action described by the verb. *Me, her, him,* and *us* are object case pronouns. *Compare to* subject case and possessive case.

object complement   An adjective that modifies the object of a sentence:

> Dew made the grass slippery.

Here *slippery* is the complement of the object *grass*. *See also* complement; *compare* subject complement.

parallel construction   The grammatical consistency of functionally or conceptually equivalent words, phrases, clauses, or sentences:

> *Correct:* We like to sing and to roller skate.

> *Incorrect:* We like singing and to roller skate.

parenthesis (plural: *parentheses*)   One of a pair of punctuation marks or a statement inserted into a train of thought that is typically placed between parentheses.

participial phrase   A phrase beginning with a participle that functions as an adverb or adjective, such as *left out, bound for glory, looking smart.*

participle verb   A form used as an adverb or adjective or to make up a whole verb together with one or more helping verbs.

passive voice   A construction in which the subject receives rather than performs the action described by the verb, such as "The cake was eaten." *Contrast* active voice.

personal pronoun   A pronoun that refers to a noun representing a person or thing: *I, he, she, it, we.*

phrase   A grouping of words that does not contain both a subject and a predicate but may function as a part of speech such as a noun, verb, adjective, or adverb. *Compare* clause.

positive form   The base form of an adjective or adverb: *green; happily. Compare* comparative form: *greener; more happily.*

possessive case   The case form that indicates that a noun or pronoun possesses a thing or quality: *mine, hers, theirs, the doctor's. Compare* subject case and object case.

predicate   Part of a sentence that specifies the action carried out by the subject. It includes the verb and may also include any words or phrases modifying the verb as well as the object of the sentence:

Her new hairdo made her look like a duck.

Here "made her look like a duck" is the predicate of the subject "her new hairdo."

preposition   A word such as *to, for, at*, and *over* that links the object to other parts of speech in a sentence.

prepositional phrase   A phrase that begins with a preposition such as *at, to, with*, and *about* and includes the preposition, its object, and any modifiers of the object: *into the briny deep; without a care in the world.*

pronoun   A part of speech that stands for a noun. *See also* personal pronoun; demonstrative pronoun; relative pronoun; interrogative pronoun; indefinite pronoun.

proper noun   The name of a one-of-a-kind person or thing, such as *Gwen* or *Eiffel Tower. Compare to* common noun.

reflexive pronoun   An object case pronoun that has the same antecedent as the subject of the sentence. *Myself, yourself, herself*, and *itself* are reflexive pronouns.

relative pronoun   A pronoun that establishes a relationship between a noun and a dependent clause that follows it. *That, which, who*, and *whom* are relative pronouns.

restrictive clause or phrase *See* essential clause or phrase.

semantics An area of language study concerned with the meaning of words.

serial comma A comma used to set apart items in a series of three or more: *you, me, the others*.

subject A part of a sentence that carries out the action described by the verb:

Roses smell nice.

Here *roses* is the subject of the sentence. *Compare* object.

subject case The form of nouns and pronouns that indicates the noun or pronoun carries out the action described by the verb. *I, you, she, we,* and *they* are subject case pronouns. *Compare* object case and possessive case.

subject complement An adjective that occurs after a linking verb and describes or restates the subject:

The sky was dark.

Here *dark* is the complement of the subject *sky*. *See also* complement; *compare* object complement.

subjunctive mood A verb form used when the action represented by the verb might not really happen:

There may be stalagmites in the cave.

Here *be* is subjunctive. *Compare* indicative mood and imperative mood.

subordinate clause *See* dependent clause.

subordinating conjunction An element that subordinates a dependent clause to an independent clause. *After, although, as, because,* and *before* are examples.

subordination   The relation and joining of two dissimilar word groups such as a clause and a phrase or a dependent and an independent clause.

superlative form   An adjectival and adverbial form used to compare three or more things. It is formed by adding *est* to the end of the base form of most adjectives and changing the *ly* ending of most adverbs to *liest*, or by using the words most or least with the adjective or adverb: *happiest; most happily*.

suspended compound   Compounded words that have an intervening word or words in the middle. They should be joined with a hanging hyphen: *mid- to upper 50s*. *See also* hanging hyphen.

syntax   An area of language study concerned with the way words fit together into larger structures.

transitive verb   Describes action that is carried out by the subject on an object:

> The scissors cut the paper.

Here *cut* is a transitive verb. *Compare* intransitive verb.

verb   A part of speech that indicates action.

verb mood   The form that makes a statement or asks a question, issues a command, or supposes a possibility. *See also* indicative mood; imperative mood; subjunctive mood.

verbals   Verb forms that may be used as nouns or adjectives. They include infinitives, gerunds, and present and past participles.

Appendix

Common Grammar Problems

The entries in this appendix define and exemplify the most frequent grammar mistakes. As noted in the individual entries, some are problems that were considered mistakes in the past but have come to be widely accepted. In contrast, one entry (generic *he*) was universally accepted until only recently. Better read fast! No one knows what changes are on the way!

comma splice The incorrect use of a comma to join two independent clauses into a single sentence:

> *Incorrect:* The accountants are taking a break again, don't they have anything better to do?

The comma should be replaced by a period.

dangling modifier A phrase without a word to modify because that word has not been stated:

> *Incorrect:* Having only just begun working, the job seemed endless.

In this example, "having only just begun working" is a dangling modifier, because the person or people who have begun are not indicated in the sentence.

> *Correct:* Having only just begun working, we felt as though the job were endless.

double comparison Redundant use of words that make comparisons, such as *more hungrier* and *most shortest*. These comparisons should be stated *hungrier* and *shortest*.

double negative Redundant use of words of negation in constructions such as "I don't want none." and "There aren't no more." These phrases should be stated, "I don't want any." and "There aren't any more."

excessive coordination The joining of too many independent clauses into a single sentence, resulting in a run-on sentence.

excessive subordination The use of too many dependent clauses to modify an independent clause, resulting in a run-on sentence.

faulty coordination The joining of two clauses that have no apparent logical relationship:

> It's chilly out today and next week the neighbors are coming over.

faulty parallelism The failure to use the same grammatical structure to express two grammatically similar words or phrases:

> *Incorrect:* I like fishing and to ride my bike.

> *Correct:* I like to fish and to ride my bike.

faulty predication An improper or illogical relationship between the subject and predicate:

> The trip home was a nice day outside.

> The reason why I eat so much is to keep up my strength.

faulty pronoun case The use of one pronoun case when another is called for, as in the confusion of *who* and *whom,* *she* and *her,* or *I* and *me.*

faulty subject-verb agreement The failure of the subject and the verb to agree in number, for example, *she deliver, we thinks, I goes.*

faulty subordination The unclear relationship between a joined dependent and independent clause:

> As long as you're doing the laundry, the dishes need washing.

fused participle Failure to use the possessive case to distinguish a noun from a participial phrase that follows it:

> *Incorrect:* We all objected to the procedure taking so long.

> *Correct:* We all objected to the procedure's taking so long.

generic *he* Use of the pronoun *he* to refer to people who may be women. Once universally accepted, the generic *he* is now widely considered sexist, as are words such as *mankind*, and gender-specific words for occupations such as *stewardess* and *salesman*. Good alternatives are *humankind, flight attendant,* and *salesperson*.

incomplete comparison The use of the comparative form of an adverb or adjective without stating two terms of comparison. This is often acceptable in casual speech but should be avoided in formal writing:

> *Incorrect:* My back is so sore.

> *Correct:* My back is so sore I can hardly sleep.

> *Incorrect:* Driving in your state is safer than mine.

> *Correct:* Driving in your state is safer than in mine.

incomplete sentence (sentence fragment) For a sentence to be complete, it must have a subject and a predicate. A single dependent clause cannot form a complete sentence.

misplaced modifiers Phrases that are badly placed, resulting in uncertainty as to which word they are intended to modify:

> *Incorrect:* I had a hard time today at city hall with the clerk trying to process my paperwork.

> *Correct:* Trying to process my paperwork at city hall today, I had a bad time with the clerk.

missing comma Failure to use a comma when it's required, especially to set apart a nonessential clause from the rest of the sentence.

passive voice Verbal construction in which the subject receives, rather than carries out, the action described by the verb:

> *Passive:* We were startled by the raccoon.

> *Active:* The raccoon startled us.

Passive voice is not incorrect, but it is frequently overused and can result in vague, flabby writing.

run-on sentence Too many clauses joined in a single sentence that should be separated into multiple sentences.

sentence beginning with a conjunction Use of *and, but, or,* or some other conjunction at the start of a sentence. This has become widely acceptable, but it was once considered inappropriate.

sentence ending with a preposition Placement of a preposition at the end of a sentence rather than before the object:

> She told us what the equipment was used for.

Contrast that with the following:

> She told us for what the equipment was used.

Prepositions at the ends of sentences were once considered mistakes but have become almost universally accepted.

shifts   Inappropriate changes in grammatical form, usually in pronoun person or number or in verb tense, that take place within a sentence or over the course of several sentences.

split infinitive   The insertion of a word immediately after *to* and before the rest of the infinitive verb form, for example, "to not care," "to boldly go," or "to always feel." Split infinitives have become widely accepted, although many sources continue to object to them.

squinting modifier   A modifier confusingly placed between two words, either of which it might be taken to modify:

> *Incorrect:* Those I relied on heavily influenced me.

> *Correct:* Those I relied on influenced me heavily.

> Or:

> *Correct:* Those I heavily relied on influenced me.

vague pronoun reference   Use of a pronoun without a clear antecedent:

> *Incorrect:* They said I could have my own office, a raise, a bonus, and an extra week's vacation. It was something I counted on.

Here the pronoun *it* could refer to any of several nouns.

Index